Praise for *In the Spirit of Home*

"In The Spirit of Home will inspire you to create a home you love. That, in turn, will help you create a life you love. Because that's how it works! And Lesley Morrison gets it. Whether you want to practice a little house magic, find your unique style, or arrange your space so energy flows in the most auspicious possible way, this book will show you how."

—Tess Whitehurst, author of *Magical Housekeeping*

in the spirit of home

About the Author

Lesley Morrison is a kitchen designer on Vancouver Island, Canada, and has been working with the world of interiors for nearly two decades. Her passion for interiors has merged with her love of nature, producing an approach to design that is both spiritual and practical. While most of her time is spent creating dream kitchens for her clients, she works closely with people looking to create meaningful spaces in and around their homes.

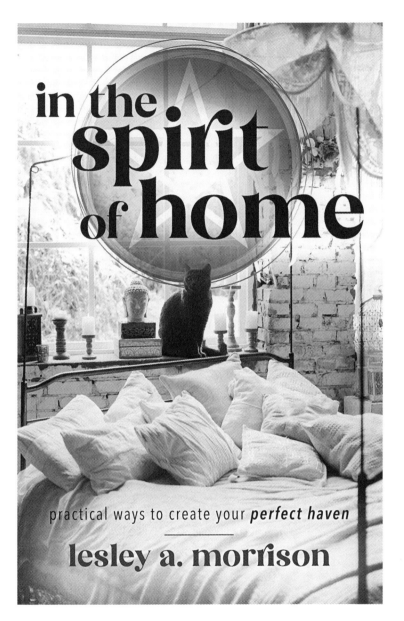

in the spirit of home

practical ways to create your *perfect haven*

lesley a. morrison

Llewellyn Publications
Woodbury, Minnesota

FIRST EDITION
First Printing, 2022

Book design by Christine Ha
Cover design by Cassie Willett

Llewellyn Publications is a registered trademark of Llewellyn Worldwide Ltd.

Library of Congress Cataloging-in-Publication Data (Pending)
ISBN: 978-0-7387-6872-4

Llewellyn Worldwide Ltd. does not participate in, endorse, or have any authority or responsibility concerning private business transactions between our authors and the public.

All mail addressed to the author is forwarded but the publisher cannot, unless specifically instructed by the author, give out an address or phone number.

Any internet references contained in this work are current at publication time, but the publisher cannot guarantee that a specific location will continue to be maintained. Please refer to the publisher's website for links to authors' websites and other sources.

Llewellyn Publications
A Division of Llewellyn Worldwide Ltd.
2143 Wooddale Drive
Woodbury, MN 55125-2989
www.llewellyn.com

Printed in the United States of America

Other Books by Lesley Morrison

The Healing Wisdom of Birds

Contents

Exercises

Introduction

....

The instinct to turn a building into a home captivates the human imagination. It drives us forward from very basic, primal needs and has made interior design and decorating one of the biggest industries in the world. Whether buying, building, or renting a home, at some point in your life re-decorating will likely be a task you undertake, for a growing family or even just for yourself. Taking the bold step to revamp your space is a rewarding undertaking, no matter what stage of life you're in, and can be the difference between living in chaos, or living your very best life. It is what we do with our space that *makes* it our home, and that is what this book is about.

As a personal design consultant and kitchen designer, I have spent many years watching clients, friends, and family struggle with making physical space meaningful, organized, and nourishing. It can be a daunting task, but with the right guidance it has the power to transform every facet of your life, inside and out. My experience in the field has shown me that many people need a more personal approach to remodeling their homes and appreciate the emphasis on smaller details rather than grand scale makeovers.

This book is about many of those smaller details. The importance of the right atmosphere, the energetic patterns that go unnoticed, the comfort of each individual room and the way it makes you feel—not just the way it turns out in a photograph.

On your journey to turning your building into a meaningful home, you will find many schools and philosophies of interior design that will bombard you with trends, formulas, ideas, and rules. This can be a good thing sometimes, because designers have spent decades making mistakes, making things awesome, and studying their predecessors to save you some serious time and money. Some popular design trends in today's modern collage are rooted deeply in very ancient religious and philosophical practices, like feng shui and Vastu Shastra. Practices like this are becoming increasingly needed to ground and balance our technological world and re-forge the bond between humanity and the natural world. But do not get too caught up in trying to follow what's on Pinterest, even though you might, like me, spend several hours of your day there (and I encourage you to do so!)

The problem with following trends, however, that I have seen from experience, is that people often neglect the deeper meaning of "home" in favor of choosing a cookie cutter design, budget friendly product, or fast and simple approach. Obviously, money is a driving factor in any house-related project, but the results often end up impersonal and lacking certain qualities of character. As a designer, I have walked into many fresh new buildings with families living inside only to be dismayed by the impression that nobody lived there at all. A house is not just a place to sleep and put our stuff, it is the place that defines your life and nurtures you and your family every day.

The foundation for this book is about creating a home that is a perfect extension, or manifestation, of what you are as an energetic being. Your home should sync up with your inner world if you are to thrive as an infinitely creative being. So, let's get started, and begin the long fun journey of finding your way home, whatever that might mean to you.

CHAPTER ONE

Finding the Right Fit

Types of Homes and What They Can Do for You

....

When I think of "home," I see a rustic cabin tucked away in the mountains with herds of deer prancing gleefully past my windows. No matter how many types of houses I design for, fall in love with, or see in magazines, the mountain home is where my heart seems to call me. Do I live in this mountain home right now? Of course not. I have a young child. I work in the city. I do not know how to ski yet and my bank account does not quite yet match the scale of my fantastical dreams.

But still. It is my dream home *idea*. It is the essence of what I find peaceful to me, and I can, at the very least, start by working those elements throughout my existing abode. Doing this reinforces the emotion behind what I want to create. If I can imagine I am living my dream life in the mountains by decorating my home like a ski chalet and backing that up with frequent trips to forest settings, I am a little bit closer already. Can you guess how many deer pictures I own?

Back to that later.

The magic is not just how it manifests, but how it feels. You won't create peace in chaotic settings, nor will you draw your wildest dreams toward you by actively ignoring their execution. So, how do you make this all happen? How do you know you're on the right path to creating your perfect and spiritually matched home?

Finding the "right fit" for a home can be either an exhilarating challenge or a no-brain-required sort of endeavor but should never be overlooked in the process of creating a spiritually optimal home. Whether you are renting or buying, the type of place you live in, its location, weather, flora and fauna can have huge impacts on your sense of belonging in this world and no matter where you are on your life's journey right now, there are wonderful ways to benefit from every type of home.

You will discover while reading this book, and in undertaking your own home journey, that many of your preferences in housing, decor, and design elements will somehow work their way back to nature. Play with this. Explore it. Your soul resonates with certain aspects of the natural world that always grab your attention when you're in need of a re-charge. Some people gravitate to the oceans, others the deep woods, and yet others the sandy deserts or tropical beaches.

Many might argue about the limitations of living in a rented space, but much can be done to brighten the spirit and open the gates of wonderful "home" energy anywhere you are and can help you inch closer to manifesting the home of your dreams in the future. I spent many of my adult years renting and enjoyed the opportunity to live in multiple kinds of homes. I know what I like, what drives me nuts, and most importantly, I understand what it is I really need in a home to make me feel at peace with my world. Many of my best interior designs were crafted and woven together in rental houses, so if you too are renting, use that as experimentation and play around with making movable magical spaces. Even if you never get the chance to buy, your home is what you put into it and should never be disregarded because your name is not on the mortgage. If you do own a family home, retirement home, or even your dream home, let the creativity flow to unleash the home you were meant for.

While this will be explored widely throughout the book, we start first by recognizing a few favorite house types on this journey to house wholeness and how to pick one that paves the foundation for your enlightened living. When "finding your way home," examine these common structures and what their designs bring to the energetic playing field and how they might impact your mood, your lifestyle, and your spiritual needs.

Cabin

Ok, yes, I just *had* to start with this one because I am unashamedly biased in its favor. One of my personal favorites, the cabin, represents all that is cozy and all that is enveloped in wilderness.

The log cabin is simple and is thought to have originated in Scandinavia and Eastern Europe where pine and spruce were readily available. They later became the preferred housing of early settlers in America and have since become modern-day retreats and luxurious getaways all over the world. The Ocean Front Village in Tofino, Canada, or the Skapet Mountain Lodges in Norway are great examples of the simple luxury a cabin getaway promises.

As a housing type, the cabin carries the energies of the simple life and an understated return to nature. If you're attracted to this housing style you probably need a break from the big wide world and are ready to elevate your need for peace and quiet. The log construction adds the grounding of the earth and forces a deep connect with nature. Whether you choose to make a cabin your main abode or a simplistic way to get away from city life, getting back to the basics of the natural world is the main idea here.

Most cottages share the same charms as the cabin, with the main difference being the construction. A cottage can be a welcome retreat from the busy urban chaos, or a primary residence, nestled anywhere from a forest by the lake to an old English hillside village.

Condo

A hallmark of urban areas, the condominium can be an affordable housing option for many people with the added perk of not having to maintain a plot of land along with it. Dating back to New York City in the year 1881[1], the condo is a great way to live in the city without the heavy upkeep of a single-family home. For those looking for a simplistic lifestyle with low upkeep, perhaps even scaling back from a larger family home, condos make good housing choices.

These housing units typically thrive in busy city centers, giving its occupants the best city life has to offer. Entertainment, dining out, and shopping might be large parts of your lifestyle if a downtown condo speaks to you. Convenience, modernity, and sometimes tremendous luxury, these clustered homes can promise high levels of energy and socialization and in the right areas are more affordable than many single-family alternatives. If connecting with others is on your spiritual itinerary, this community-oriented building type could be the choice for you. Condo living can also mean focusing more time on career, travel, or retirement, and less time on lawn care. If deciding on condo living take your design cues from the

....

1. Lasner, Matthew, *High Life: Condo Living in the Suburban Century* (New Haven, CT: Yale University Press, 2012).

surrounding environment and try to work some of the architectural features and landscape into your perfect haven.

Single-Family Home

The most popular home choice around the world, single-family dwellings promise oodles of space to grow that family tree. Thoughts of hot cocoa around the fire and camping out in the backyard under the open stars spring to mind. With options from two bedrooms and up, anything is possible here. If this style of home is on your radar, you are probably looking to enjoy an expanding family or simply to enjoy the freedom and control of your own space.

Having your own property encourages family gatherings, large garden spaces and backyards for barbeques. Freedom is the biggest advantage of this housing no matter what stage of life you're in and whether you rent or own. From small rancher style homes to regal manor houses, it can be a peaceful place for your family to call home.

These homes do carry larger upkeep and long-term care, but the rewards of having a house large enough for a family to grow usually far outweigh the burdens of regular maintenance. If you're craving longevity, whether suburban, out in the country, or up in the mountains, a single-family home is probably your best bet, and design possibilities are endless here.

Apartment

Apartments are great for experimenting with "movable" design, but often pose the most challenge for those with modest budgets. Living small, however, has many advantages! Do not skimp on the niceties just because you're renting, though. Use these opportunities to play around with decor ideas and get a taste of what styles and trends appeal to you. Remember, you can always take your cozy apartment with you when you upgrade to another home so do not be afraid to let loose with the curtains and throw pillows. Many of my favorite images from Pinterest are of perfectly styled apartments—so you have no excuse not to give it your best shot. One of my youngest clients transformed her first apartment into a plant paradise and we let loose the opportunity to showcase some of her long-collected treasures from her teenager years at home. When first leaving home, my son did the very same thing and made his small rental suite a cozy place to store a book collection and an army of succulents.

EXERCISE
Home-Finding Activity

All right, it's list time!

I love lists, and what better way to narrow down those house and home goals than to write them down. Answer these questions when deciding on where to settle down, either before or after the following meditation exercise:

Do I enjoy outdoor space?

Can I maintain a garden and/or yard?

Would I need the space outdoors (kids, entertaining, pets, etc., now or in the future?)

Your short, and long-term goals are important here. Consider whether you're likely to have a large family and the time to maintain an outdoor space. If you're a gardener, apartments and condos likely won't fulfill some necessary spiritual needs.

Do I like noise?

Do I actively close windows at the first utterings of children playing outside?

Do I want to hear other people's doors closing all day long? These are questions I keep at the top of my list and are crucial for lasting peace. If you do not like to see and hear your neighbor's day in and day out, then condos / apartments are probably not for you. Many new single-family home developments in highly urbanized areas are crammed together also, so make sure you keep the hustle and bustle of other people, as well as street traffic, in mind when choosing your new home

Finally, will I be commuting daily for work? Do I need or enjoy the convenience of take-out food, pubs, malls, and movie theaters? If you're the kind of person who can sustain a lifestyle outside the city borders, then the sky is the limit when home hunting.

EXERCISE
Meditation for Finding Your New Home

All of these housing choices might be overwhelming at first, especially when trying to accommodate things like budget, location, or the needs of children, but you can tap into your inner design guru to lead you to the right property or make the very best of a home you already occupy. Try this meditation to align your current housing wants and needs with what the universe actually wants for you— even if that means staying exactly where you are and transforming your current space into more of your dream space.

Trust me on this one—sometimes we stumble onto our best accommodation when we stop looking for it.

Before you begin—get comfortable. Go pee. Pajama pants on. Bra off (if applicable). Sit in your favorite chair or meditation cushion or bed and shake off the day. Breathe in and out ten times, and with each breath imagine a fragment of your day floating off with it back into the cosmos like a feather in the wind. Find your center and be still in the moment you're in.

Now that you're relaxed, allow an image to come to mind of what kind of home you want. Be generous here. Lavish swimming pool perhaps, five bedrooms, nine bathrooms, tennis courts, prancing deer. Let all of your heart's desires pour into this exercise. Breathe in and out slowly while you picture your dream home in your mind's eye.

Now stop. Let all of that dissolve. Let it fade into darkness and send it back into the cosmos. This is the crucial part where you break apart your gimme, gimme, gimme expectations. Yes, I mean it. This is the magical step that allows what you really *need* into your sphere of creation. By letting go of ideals that could limit a manifestation, an open mind and heart will allow opportunity to start trickling into your life. Start feeling the joy and acceptance of living in peace. Feel the serenity of a country home, or the excitement of downtown city life, or the heart warming of large family gatherings. Allow the *essence* of what you want to fill your being, rather than weighing it down with the fine print.

This is not to say that you shouldn't have the basic idea of what you want when you begin. That is still an important step. But instead of thinking *condo with full ocean views and granite counters and across from Denny's within my budget,* allow the idea of a condominium lifestyle to have its place but ditch the preconceived notions of the small details. Try focusing on how your perfect house match would make you feel instead of what it will give you.

Now say quietly, or in your mind: *I release all expectation and allow the universe to guide me to my perfect home.*

Repeat this mantra daily, each time noticing any recurring feelings, memories, or new ideas that may give you clues as to what direction you are being pulled. Remember, there is nothing wrong with a more direct and active approach, but this mindfulness can open new avenues in your search for a home that you may not have recognized.

In my own experience, coveting a house in the mountains I continually find myself in homes surrounded by trees and wildlife, but always within the convenience of suburban settings (ugh, fine, universe! You win again). Some things become ingrained so deeply that it's hard to manifest outside of them, and this is entirely the point! But it is also good practice to make sure these things are lining up with the way of life that serves your true spiritual purpose.

However you find your home, give thanks for the newness it offers and put your best energies into making it your own. Now it's time to get to work turning your place into a perfect haven.

CHAPTER TWO

Feng Shui and the Art of Perfect Placement

....

Many people are familiar with the ancient practice of feng shui in some form or another due to its widespread popularity all over the world. If you're not, feng shui is a unique way of arranging spaces in harmony with the natural world and has been incorporated into interior design and architecture for decades. Translating to "wind-water" in English, feng shui is also known as Chinese geomancy and has been in practice for well over 3000 years. While a popular and ongoing modern-day trend in the design universe, the origins of feng shui are rooted in early Taoism, a philosophy developed out of a deep belief in cosmic balance maintained and regulated by *chi*, a divine force that flows through everything in existence.

Chi animates matter, giving life to all things. It is the primal energy that moves in and out of our bodies, and in and around our homes. In the Taoist tradition, a person is taught to "go with the flow" and connect to the space around them in meaningful ways. These are the foundational ideas behind what we see today when a designer must decide where to place the furniture and what shade of paint to use in the bedrooms. Because this chi is ever flowing and powerful its ability to sustain and transform life must be respected. Blocking this life force usually creates spaces and circumstances that lead to mental, emotional, and spiritual fatigue but is easy to remedy when you have the right information.

Originally used to orient sacred structures, dwellings, and other buildings for the most auspicious outcomes, feng shui is a hot topic for interior design books all on their own. It embraces the harmony of the universe and finds practical ways to arrange structural space while helping you attract more of the positive things you want and warding off those things not beneficial to your ongoing health and happiness. You can find almost endless resources both in books and in blog posts about the fascinating history of this tradition, but in this chapter, I am going to briefly discuss some of the most important aspects for each room as it relates to the goal of this book—creating a spiritually optimal home.

But first, some core feng shui principles to help you along on your journey.

The Elements

Lying at the heart of ancient Greek cosmology, the four elements of matter were believed to comprise everything in the universe. Earth, water, air, and fire were the center of philosophy, science and medicine for two thousand years and is still how we categorize the world of matter today in the Western world.

Even in the beginnings of philosophical discovery, each element was given traits that represented certain aspects of physical life. The elements have been used to classify many things over the centuries, even personalities, and have been recognized and given spiritual significance all over the world. Within the domain of paganism, these four elements are honored as sacred and play an important role in ritualistic magic and almost every aspect of traditional pagan and Neo-pagan beliefs. Each element is also associated with a direction on the compass.

Within the parameters and philosophy of feng shui, these same elements make up a perfectly harmonized home, together with metal, and ensure the correct distribution of chi. Each element has a direction, a purpose, and a specific set of patterns that are believed to influence certain areas of not just your home, but your entire life.

Interior design and architecture in all of its guises and schools makes great use of the elements, in fact, and their ideal workings in tangible space. While it is most notably discussed within the framework of feng shui, many designers pay close attention to the interactions of the natural world and find ways to incorporate the elements.

Because all of the elements are used and celebrated throughout different design schools and spiritual practices, we will look at all of their historical meanings and applications within feng shui, and outside of it. Design is, after all, adaptable and bendable and should allow for differing perspectives.

Once you get a glimpse of what each element can do for your home and garden, see what works best for you and your personal space with some trial and error. If you're a Virgo like me, you know earth and wood elements are crucial for your happiness, but a water type might feel more peaceful with a stronger application of water— well-grounded with other more substantial elements. Whichever element inspires you the most, make sure you keep it balanced to avoid blockages down the road.

Earth

Nothing would get far without the earth, and it is an element of pure, primal power. A strong force in any application, earth is secure and solid, full of endurance and life-giving force. Associated with the North, the element earth is considered a feminine power representing the mother goddess in her most nurturing aspect.

Symbolically, earth roots humanity to material sustenance, abundance and healthy connections to our sacred ancestry and creates the foundations required to thrive as physical beings. It is the materialization of all our desires as made tangible on the physical plane. Earth is the grounding of spirituality and higher guidance being put into action through our bodies.

In feng shui, earth brings in these grounding qualities and is considered receptive and formative. In proper feng shui design this element nourishes and creates stability and keeps more unstable elements such as water under control. Earth creates feelings of trust, security, and a comfort in the good things life has to offer. Without the right amount of this element, your life may become flighty, restless, anxious, and prone to discontent. A lack of the earth element in the home can make the path forward a daunting one and goals scattered in too many directions.

When looking to incorporate the earth element into a design plan, there are several things you can do to boost this energy. You can choose earth tones for wall colors like beige, taupe, or sand in rooms that fall under the influence of the earth element. If you are working with a new build or a larger renovation, brick and tiles are perfect choices to represent earth, either on the floor or on the walls and can be built into a new design.

Terra-cotta planters are also great additions, or any other earthenware pottery. The colors of these rustic looking pieces can also be incorporated into a space to add earth element energy as a feature wall or an accessory like pillows or blankets.

Crystals and rocks add great earth energy to the home as well and add interest anywhere you put them. Try adding a bowl of your favorite stones to a coffee table or a prized chunk of natural quartz or a salt lamp beside your bed. You could also add statues made from stone, stone lamps , or other architectural features. Working in the garden is another fantastic way to feed the power and energy of the earth element into your daily life.

Water

Much like earth, water is crucial to life as we know it. Water, it could be said, connects everything on the planet, for there is nothing alive on this Earth that does not need water to survive. From bacteria to blue whales, water keeps life moving in a steady stream of abundant existence.

Symbolically, water is the most receptive and feminine of all the elements and has long represented the emotions, intuition, imagination, and the subconscious realms. Water can be both gentle and powerful, sometimes trickling along the path of least resistance or rushing headlong with strength and determination. In its gentle state, water does not struggle against obstacles but rather goes around them. In its destructive state, water has the power to destroy entire villages.

In many traditions water is a healing element with great powers of transformation and cleansing. Many forms of life use water to bathe in, while still many others call it home.

Influenced by the waxing and waning of the moon, water is considered a magical element and belongs, in many pagan circles, to the mother goddess and her life-giving attributes—much like the earth.

In the practice of Wicca, water is represented by the cauldron or chalice and symbolizes the womb from which life is born. Humanity has always held a special reverence for water, so its use in home design for creating a spiritually optimized space is widely explored all over the world.

In interior design water is often incorporated to create a sense of flow through a space. In feng shui, the water element represents wealth, abundance, and career success. These being important to many people, the water element should be applied properly and kept in check. Too much water in the home can create a "wishy-washy" temperament and the inability to root firmly and make solid decisions. While it is true that water can help form dreams, ideals, and fantasies, without the grounding of other elements like earth or wood, water would keep us in a state of perpetual daydreaming with no real dedication to creating what we want in the physical world.

Water's restorative effects, though, help add the qualities of relaxation and serenity to your peaceful abode and can be excellent allies if you're retired, recovering from illness or injury, or live a hectic lifestyle and need a reminder to slow down a bit. Many people enjoy the luxuries of deep soaker bathtubs, hot tubs, pools and rain shower features in their homes which is evidence of how much we rely on water for comfort and nurturing on a very regular basis at every stage of life.

To bring water into your home effectively, a water feature is always a great choice. A tabletop fountain can be added to a water sector in the home or garden and can enhance the positive flow of chi in your career and bank account. The color black most often represents the water element in feng shui, but you can also use deeper shades of navy blue. Mirrors also stand in for the water element due to their reflective qualities, as do images with wavy lines or patterns.

Go for items that have a fluid texture, or even a framed print or painting of calm water.

Fire

Fire is an exciting element and one of the most dynamic energies to work with. It is the giver of light and is usually seen as the representation of romance, passion, inspiration, and vitality. It is the force and power of the sun that nourishes all life and the warmth that gets us through the coldest of winters.

The energy of fire can be completely uplifting and elevate our personal energy as well as our ability to get where we want in life. Common sayings like "light a fire under it," or "set fire to" are used often to express a sudden burst of motivation and determination, reminding us of a subconscious wisdom of this element and its intrinsic capacity for action. The element of fire also holds the innate power to invigorate a tired spirit, opening a creative mind back up to expression after periods of dormancy or a general lack of ambition. The heat of fire can signal a thirst for achievement and is predominantly an active energy. Many things get done when we embrace the fire element, for it is a strong and purposeful ally when directing our personal will and intentions. Courage, too, comes from this element, and the will necessary to carry out arduous, challenging and even dangerous tasks.

Not surprisingly, fire is also quick to anger and is often aggressive in its potency and should be balanced properly with the other elements. Those with large tempers are said to have fiery personalities and an overabundance of the fire element in one's life and home should be remedied when possible.

From a metaphysical perspective, fire has both the power to create and destroy and has always been treated with respect in spiritual and religious traditions. Fire is transformative in its ability to burn away the dead or dying aspects of our lives to make room for new growth. Often, we pass through years of our lives clinging onto the same routines, thoughts, relationships, and life goals that perhaps have no real meaning for us anymore. Fire is a crucial element in helping us clear away this underbrush and focus on moving forward with a clear path ahead. The legendary story of the phoenix rising from its own ashes after bursting into flames is a perfect way of understanding the role of fire in the growth and development of the spirit on its journey. Symbolically, fire is a catalyst for intense change.

In feng shui, the fire element is believed to enhance one's reputation and fame when applied in the correct areas of the home. Fire in the form of candles or a cozy open fireplace are wonderful ways to introduce this element into the home and create both comfort and elemental balance. It is a common practice in the world of interior design to make the fireplace a focal point of the room because whether a living room, master bedroom, bathroom or kitchen, an open fire tugs at very primitive memories in the human psyche and reminds us of our basic needs upon the planet.

The colors of the fire element can also be added to brighten up a room and invite more of the warmth and vigor needed to enhance this sector. Reds, oranges, and yellows work well, and as I will discuss later in the chapter on color meanings, fiery colors often produce higher energies in the physiological and emotional arenas.

Air

Air is the element of the mind and carries the energies of freedom, space, new possibilities, and imagination. Many people might not see the connections between interior design and the element of air, but the very space you occupy and imprint yourself upon is made up of this element. Air also governs dreams, ideas, wishes, and all the inspiration you have gathered when you start your home design or redecorating projects. For this reason, air has come to symbolize communication on all levels, whether from yourself *to* yourself, or wafting in from some divine source. The element of air is what your thoughts are up to and speaks directly of your mental clarity as well as your ability to transform your thoughts into words or actions.

When looking for ways to bring some of the magic of air into your space, think about your relationship with it. Do you talk a lot and listen little? Do you exercise, increasing oxygen to your cells? Do you open windows daily—even in cold weather—for a blast of fresh outside air to come in? Meditation and controlled breathing exercises are fantastic ways to work with the element of air and burning herbs or incense will invite the magic through your space whenever you use it with the right intentions.

To find a deeper connection with the air element, I always recommend watching the little beings who inhabit the air on a regular basis. I am a well-known bird fan and often have images of birds around my home as well as a very successful bird-friendly garden. Birds are well connected to the air element, both environmentally and spiritually, and will provide some excellent feedback as to how to work with it in your own life. Spend time birdwatching and notice the expansiveness around you and the limitless space that is open for dreams and ideas just waiting to take form.

When planning your interior space, think about how air moves around from room to room. In feng shui, there is no category of the element of air, but rather the term chi, or qi that we work so hard to keep flowing around us. Vaulted ceilings will heighten the experience of open space, as will large windows and skylights uninhibited by heavy drapery. Be mindful also of how much you cram into a room and pay close attention to the way people move around furniture with each layout you try.

There is a delicate balance, however, between this open sense of space and feeling too exposed. Your home must create the comfort of being safe and protected and for most people there is a need to "hide" from the outside world—at least some of the time. Too much empty space, or space not well utilized can make your home seem unlived in. Remember to ground that flighty air energy into meaningful arrangements of furniture and personal treasures.

Wood

As an element, wood signals the joys and unlimited potential of the springtime, upward growth, and new life. Wood is expansive, durable, and encourages hope and idealism. While earth is the element that creates your solid foundation and roots you firmly into the ground, it is wood that sustains the ongoing momentum of the new bud opening into the world to fulfill its purpose.

When we reflect on trees, we can see the enduring fascination and importance of this element in our everyday lives. Although strongly planted in the ground, trees reach upward to the heavens while bending and swaying with the wind. Wood is a movement-oriented element, and so does well in areas designed for work or creativity. It has the patience for hard work and the stamina to continuously reach for the sun even on the cloudy days.

Wood is also soothing, so surrounding your home with living plants will activate this element in its most natural form. Tending and caring for plants is a fundamental practice for staying connected to the physical world and has been known to have some stellar effects on the spiritual body as well.

And if you do go plant crazy, as many of us do when we first start out, make sure they are well tended and that you have the time and energy to give them. A dying plant is not going to boost your home's chi. If you're one of those folks who wasn't gifted a green thumb, go for occasional fresh cut flowers, pictures or paintings with pastoral scenes, or even a wallpaper with a vibrant green leaf pattern.

Interior design trends have a lot of fun with the wood element, and many of today's most popular schematics involve the use of heavy, rustic wood accents. *Rustic* and *country* styles focus mainly on wood for furniture, walls, ceiling beams, and even home construction and should be explored if you are hoping to find creative ways to add the wood element into your new or existing home. Wood is a fairly masculine energy, however, and should be balanced out with some softer textiles for the best impact. Pair your heavier wood furniture with metal and soft materials on sofas, chairs, and ottomans.

Metal

Metal is an element of perfect clarity, precision, freshness, and structure. It expresses simplicity and is often seen in modern, sleek designs as a step away from heavy looking architecture and toward a cleaner aesthetic. Today's most popular design trends involve the dynamic use of metals commonly used as exterior building materials indoors. Steel paneling and corrugated metal sheets are all making a splash, while the ongoing merging of metals with rustic woods captures a harmonious relationship between these two vital elements in home design. When using the principles of feng shui, however, it is believed that metal weakens wood, so avoid metal wherever you are trying to increase the energy of the wood element.

Many homes are already abundant in the metal element, especially those where walls have been painted white or the kitchen has been given the all-white makeover. The color white is the best way to bring the metal element in to play and instills a sense of peace, cleanliness, and perfection. Gray is another color that expresses the energy of metal and makes a great companion for white shades and wood tones.

To add some metal energy into the home, think metal lamps, accent tables, windchimes, bells, mirrors, and picture frames made of metal. Circular shapes are also considered to represent metal, and any artwork with metal in the imagery—like the Eiffel Tower—will carry its energy.

Feng Shui Principles

The foundation of feng shui for design and architecture is creating and maintaining the correct flow of chi. This energy can be manipulated by good placement, good cleaning practices, as well as the proper use of all five elements.

Even outside of the application of traditional feng shui, good energy can be brought into the home with the same dedication to order, balance, intention, and placement, but because this very ancient philosophy ties in so closely with this book's idea of creating a spiritually optimized home, let's investigate some of the more well-known principles at work and how you can use them in the broader scale of your home re-design project.

Keep in mind that there are hundreds of in-depth sources of feng shui on the market and on the web, and this is only meant as a brief overview. If you decide to go more detailed in the direction of feng shui, do your research and pick up some dedicated literature on the subject. I have studied feng shui only personally and occasionally as a designer and in no way consider myself an expert on the subject.

The Bagua

The *bagua*, translating to "eight areas," is the feng shui energy map and is usually where you will begin the feng shui adventure of your home. It is an ancient tool used within the feng shui philosophy to reveal where certain aspects of your life are expressed most dramatically in your home and what elements will guide those energy centers. It is the most systematic and effective way to evaluate your home and the dynamic way energy is moving around in your environment.

There are many layers to the bagua, and different applications of its use depending on the school of feng shui you are using. The map is meant to be laid over the floorplan of a home, building, or individual room to locate the governing energies of each specific place. Once you have located the eight energy centers in your space you can start activating them by using the correct elemental energies associated with each. Here are the eight sections of every building and room, and a brief breakdown of their attributes.

Wealth and Prosperity

Located in the upper left corner (southeast) of your home, this section governs your family's material wealth and investments, and your ability to locate new sources of financial income. The element here is wood and its associated colors are green and blue. Healthy plants are great boosters here, and water will enhance the energy of wood in this sector.

Fame and Reputation

Located in the rear south part of your home (south), this section is all about your public acclaim—or desire for it—and the material rewards for all your hard work. Ruled by the element of fire, this is where you want your vibrant reds and summery decor. An image of the sun is a great boost for the reputation sector, adding the vitality of this element to your ability to achieve far reaching success and recognition.

Love and Marriage

Located in the rear right corner of your home (southwest), this section rules our most personal and romantic undertakings and our luck manifesting love and passion in our lives. Governed by earth, this section does well with earth elements such a pottery and rocks/crystals, as well as the colors white, pink, and red. Objects in this sector of the home, or bedroom, should be in pairs to represent partnership.

Children and Creativity

Located in the west of your home, this is where the energy of children and creative endeavors like to shine. If you're an artist or author, this is the area of the home, or a room, to focus on for creative flow and inspiration. Those hoping to expand their family should activate this area as well with playful, youth like imagery.

Its primary element is metal and the best colors to use are white, metal, and gold/yellow.

Health and Family

Located in the east of the home, this section governs the health and vitality of you and your family. The east also represents new growth, springtime, and renewal. Its element is wood, and healthy plants are good activators here. Go for green, blue, and turquoise in your color additions and enhance the strong wood energy with water. A small fountain or the color black will nurture the wood element and help the slow growth of new life.

Knowledge and Self Cultivation

Located in the lower front corner of your home (northeast), this area focuses on personal growth, spiritual progress, and the quest for inner wisdom. It also directs our intentions toward learning new skills and information and activating this section of the home will boost studies and academic pursuits of all kinds. The knowledge and wisdom sector of the home is ruled by the element earth, so all earth colors and materials will enhance the productivity of learning endeavors and aspirations.

Career and Life Path
Located in the north, this part of the home rules your career success and life path fulfillment. This area is governed by the element water and is important for creating opportunity for growth and achievement in your chosen field. Any water feature will boost and activate the career area of the home or office, as will the colors black and blue, or any imagery of water. Mirrors also act as water due to their reflective abilities and can enhance the chi in the north.

Helpful People and Travel
Located in the northwest, or bottom right corner of the home, this is the area that governs mentors, guides and worldly adventures. This section boosts your chances of meeting the right people at the right time and getting the attention of people in positions of influence. It can also bring you international attention and success overseas. Its element is big metal, so try adding metal objects here, or anything that moves regularly like a television, clock, or even a fan. Add in some earth element touches, as earth enhances the strength of metal in this sector.

Health and Center
Located in the center of your home, this section holds all of the other centers together in harmony. Governed by the strong earth element, this part of the home is your foundation and should be kept orderly and well maintained. Depending on what room or space lies at the center of your home, you may need to implement some cures to keep the chi flowing.

EXERCISE
Mapping It All Out

Bringing the power of feng shui into your home can be a rewarding endeavor, but needs a solid framework, or game plan, to get started. Being a very old tradition, some of the principles can be complex, but if you're a beginner you'll want to decide which school of feng shui you're going to follow and how best to map out your home—wherever you're living. Remember, feng shui is a way of living with continually moving energy and applies to every building and every space everywhere.

The first bagua, or energy map, is the one used in classical feng shui. This bagua relies on compass directions to accurately map out your space and determine the influences of each quadrant of the home. The second school, called BTB, was introduced to the west by Master Lin Yun and has since become a popular and well-used tradition in the world of interiors.

Some experts propose that the bagua used in classical feng shui is the only correct way to map a space, while many others suggest using the one that feels right and empowers you to positively transform any space.

Now for the exercise:

Step One: Pick a map. Whichever one you decide to use, place it over a floorplan of your home to layout the corresponding elemental energies that are going to guide your placements, decor, and overall foundation for each part of your home and/or each individual room.

Step Two: Make a list. When you know what each quadrant requires based on its elemental correspondence, make a list of possible items that will represent each of them. You will likely find that you already own home decor that fits into most of the above discussed elemental groups, and simple placement adjustment or rearrangement will make great changes very quickly.

You do not need to go out and spend a fortune on new things, unless that is the scope of your project, nor do you need those specific feng shui objects (money frog, fu dogs, Chinese coins) if they do not fit into your overall design. The bottom line I always suggest to my clients is to never buy anything you do not connect with, even in the case of feng shui. There are many easy ways to make your home harmonious and bring those elements together by just looking at the space in a new perspective.

Step Three: Put it to practice. When you have your game plan set, work with one room at a time. Use a compass if you're following the classical tradition and watch for areas where there might be clutter or stagnant energy patterns. I recommend using the space clearing tips in the next chapter before mapping out your home for feng shui enhancements, and really take your time to connect with the natural flow of your home before you start moving furniture.

A home that has good flowing chi will feel right, and you may find that not all the techniques and suggestions offered by feng shui work for your life. The basic principles of harmonious placement, however, will have a tremendous impact on your clarity, health, and sense of purposeful living.

CHAPTER THREE

Clearing Spaces

The Magic of Letting It Go (Or Kicking It Out)

....

Everything that happens is a result of energy. This is no longer a fact that any reasonable human being can deny, so I will assume you, the reader, are a reasonable human being. In the scientific community, the law of conservation states that energy cannot be created or destroyed, but only changed from one form to another.[2] We can observe this same principal in our daily lives by paying attention to how we convert our own personal energy in the form of emotional responses, as well as physical and mental activities.

Here is an example:

Suppose for some reason I yell at you because you almost crashed into my new car. You will likely feel anger in return, maybe frustration and embarrassment, and soak up the energetic lashing I gave you like a sponge without any knowledge of it whatsoever. You will

....

2. Ethan Boechler, et al., "Energy Education: Law of conservation of energy," last updated Septemeber 27, 2021, https://energyeducation.ca/encyclopedia/Law_of_conservation_of_energy.

probably then take that anger home with you, or to work, and perhaps yell at someone else, or slam a door, to find a way of releasing the negative vibes I threw your way earlier in your day. For the anger to go away, it must be changed, or redirected altogether. Another approach might be to consciously release the emotion by meditating, breathing it away, or visualizing it leaving our energetic aura entirely. By doing this, we have changed its path and given it new direction and new purpose with the added benefit of not creating further negative responses. We are constantly taking energy from one thing and placing it toward another. That is how paintings are painted and stories are written and all of creation perpetuates itself.

So how does this apply to your house and home?

Very easily.

Without the proper interventions, patterns of energy tend to bind experiences. Strong emotions or thoughts, such as anger or love, are like gorilla glue, sticking to the walls and capturing whatever crosses its path.

Clearing space is an important step when seeking to transform a home into a better, more spiritually optimal place. Unless a home is being built brand new, there will always be residues of past experiences lingering like cobwebs in any home you move into. You will need to arm yourself with some remedies and tricks for getting rid of unwanted *stuff* to pave the foundation for a sanctuary devoid of energetic leftovers.

Let's start first with the easy part: the "stuff" you can actually see.

Part One: Closet Control — Cleaning That Which Hides

This section is meant to help you get started, get motivated, and get the garbage gone. Gather your boxes and roll up your sleeves because you're going to donate like you've never donated before.

But how do you know if you have a problem with "stuff"? How can you tell the difference between uncontrollably *collecting*, or just plain *unorganized*? There is a fine line between keeping things of value, stored safely in a garage or attic, and just piling up stuff you cannot be bothered to do anything about. But on your life's journey to homeward bliss, you need to be painfully honest about which category your "stuff" fits into.

Keeping things around that hold no value is not healthy.

But why? Why is it a bad idea to keep something around you *may* need later in life but can never actually be sure you will?

Giving into this type of thought pattern keeps you locked unnecessarily in the future. You are binding yourself to a world of "what if's" instead of being in tune with your present reality. A broken refrigerator is a broken refrigerator, and if you think you may get around to fixing it one day, you're living way ahead of your current state of affairs. This is also true of old baby clothes that somebody in the family may need one day in twenty years, or the plant that died weeks ago but "may start sprouting" again next year. I had a client many years ago that kept very dead plants in the garden in the hopes they would come back to life if left to nature. The brown leaves made her sad each time she saw them but ripping them up seemed to her like failure. Needless to say, it was an unhealthy frame of mind fueled by a guilt of being unable to care for them. Once they finally came out with a little coaxing, and she acquired some newfound skills in the garden, she was a much happier person.

This type of mentality comes from some very interesting internal processes, one that focuses on the future, and the other on the past. "I would rather hang on to this in case I ever find a spot for it." "I should keep the old toaster in case the new one breaks down." "I should keep the kid's artwork for another ten years in case they ever want to see it."

These are the kinds of ways we talk ourselves into not letting go. The kids do not care about their baby stuff anymore than your future self will care about that broken fridge. Of course, there may be some sentimentality involved, or guilt about releasing some part of your life. Your "things" can often define stages of life through memories.

But to truly live in the present and invite new energies in, you need to make a clear choice to sort the clutter and move on.

How?

I will tell you.

First, make those piles you always hear about on the organizing shows: donate, trash, keepsake. It's okay to have things from the past, but make sure they genuinely have a place in your life before storing them for another fifty years. When my mother died, I thought I should keep everything she owned. Because I had lost her, I had to keep her essence in the form of slippers and pillowcases, right?

Wrong.

After many months of cleaning, I kept her birth certificate, her death certificate, and a few of my favorite photos of her throughout her life, all kept neatly in an envelope and tucked away, or displayed nicely in a couple of frames (the photos, not death papers). Donating her things was like waking up from a heavy dream and let new life back in to my own again. Do not keep burdens out of necessity, but rather just the things that serve as simple reminders of a joy once lived.

Next, send those non-sentimental items to the thrift shops where they may just be someone else's treasure. Most second-hand shops are charitable organizations so you will be benefiting in more than one way, not to mention freeing up valuable space in your home *and* your psyche. Even the broken stuff, like that fridge that won't work or those chairs with missing slats, can be repurposed by the right person. Send them all on their merry way so you can begin anew and in the now.

Scientists and designers alike have studied clutter for decades, and the general consensus is that clutter agitates, disrupts, and keeps our minds from focusing on other things. Living with clutter is a lingering job that never gets done and most healthy adults find stress is not getting a job done. I have had friends who dreaded going home after work because of the mess they faced each night and, although an alarming concept, is not hard to understand when you have kids, pets, and a full-time career. When you get a handle of what's there, however, you can take back control of your home and turn it into the restful abode you were destined to create. If you're going to make your home an extension of you and a place for growth, peace, and joy, the job *has* to get done. Do not even think about buying new furniture and curtains until this step has been completed and you have received your gold star.

When going through the motions of what to keep and what to toss, set yourself specific parameters. Ask yourself the following questions:

1. Does it have a purpose? If the things piled in the closets or heaped in the drawers are useful for your everyday living, they should be out in the main living space and being used regularly. I once kept a massage pillow designed for the bathtub for six years, moved homes with it twice, and never used it because it did not stick to the tub. I realized one day enough was enough and into the donation box it went.

If you're not using something, it is not serving your life and needs to go.

This same philosophy applies to treadmills that hold laundry and weights that hold doors open. Reassess your space and be realistic about your daily routines.

2. Is it in good shape? Keeping things that are broken can dampen your energy over time. Bedding with stains and holes can make you feel tired. Dishes with cracks and chips can take away from the nourishment you derive from a good meal. Athletic equipment that is outworn may not give you the benefits you're looking for. If what you're using has lost its luster, it's time to give it the old heave ho!

3. Does it make me happy? Does it fit my present self? These are big ones, and nothing should stay in your humble home without passing these tests. The hallmark of Marie Kondo's tidying up philosophy, this is the true test of not only the state of your house, but the state of your spirit.

Clothes that make you feel overweight and out of shape will not make you happy. Pictures, jewelry, or other items from past relationships probably do not fit with your current self. Piles of old bills and reminders of past debts might keep you reliving less than perfect days gone by.

If anything in your home brings about feelings of stress, resentment, sadness, or inner turmoil (we will exclude family members here), then it's definitely time to say goodbye. In an ideal home environment, you should be surrounded by things that bring about fond memories, inspire dreams, encourage your best energy, and soothe your soul.

Now that you've paired down the stuff, it's time to get it organized. The air should feel lighter already, and some people say they feel like they've dropped ten pounds of weight after a good decluttering. Most of that weight probably comes from psychological attachment. The good news is that organizing and maintaining a home free of unnecessary junk is relatively easy. You might find strange things happening, like everything seems to have a place, all your daily items fit into drawers, and you may be able to store your clothes in the closet and dresser without the need to bring in storage totes and heavy-duty shoe organizers. This last one's a bit dicey and unlikely, but miracles *can* happen!

So where do you start when re-aligning your home for optimal space management? Start by finding a system that works for you and the space available in your home. If you live in small quarters, think about multipurpose furniture pieces, such as trunks and benches that can double as seating or tables. Murphy beds are a popular choice for tiny dwellings, and bunkbeds are a great idea to free up available floor space. Think more about built-in styles if you're cramped for space and utilize some of today's best space saving ideas that are being used for tiny home design.

Collections

For those of you that genuinely *collect* things, like cool rocks, shells and sticks, crystals, taxidermy, deer pictures, or Captain America memorabilia, there are great ways to showcase your stuff without your house looking like a yard sale. This is also a fine line, by the way, as I have experienced with more than one client in my career. You may think you can never have enough crystal vases, but you might be terribly wrong.

Designate a special cabinet, bookcase, or wall for your collection. Doing so will have a bigger impact from a design perspective, and visually it makes more sense than just laying bits and pieces around the house as you find them. Your guests shouldn't have to go on a scavenger hunt to see your unique interests unfold. One of my clients, an avid collector of succulents, chose to make a brilliant display for her plant babies on an old wooden ladder strapped safely to the wall adjacent to the front door. Not only did they get direct light through the skylight, but the immediate sight of the display upon walking inside was inspiring.

Avoid hanging onto pieces that are chipped or otherwise imperfect unless you can realistically repair them. While I too sometimes enjoy the "flea market" style of beloved used treasures and furnishings, make sure you can refurbish what you find into something both pleasing to look at and meaningful to possess.

Organization

Alongside common sense, proper and well thought out storage solutions will be your best allies here. Utilize closets and dressers to keep clothing out of sight. If you're using laundry baskets to hold "spill over" clothing, then you might have a problem. Go back to the start and donate, then shut closet door. The end.

In the kitchen, you have endless options for keeping your daily gadgets in check. As a kitchen designer, my clients usually ask me about the organizers first and these are often the best use of the budget. Pull out garbage and recycling bins are amazing, keeping the sight and smell of waste away from your chronic attention. Cutlery dividers are always a good investment, keeping your utensils in better shape and allowing for smoother, more joyful food prep experiences because you're not getting angry trying to find the paring knife.

Remember—simplicity is key when organizing your home. It should make sense and flow with the way you live.

Now you're ready for the next part of your adventure.

Part Two: Aura Control — Clearing What You Cannot See

For those of you that passed part one, congratulations! Here is your gold star.

But that was just the easy part, no matter how many tears and doubts came along with it. Now I am going to teach you how to clear away stuff you *can't* see and probably do not even know is there. Sounds like a fun way to spend a weekend, doesn't it? Chasing unseen dirt with a spiritual feather duster.

As mentioned before, homes being newly built won't have the residuals of past owners hanging on for dear life and only require phases of part one (unless you're in the unfortunate position where you've built a house over a graveyard). Homes previously lived in, however, have many stories to tell—both good and bad—and should be cleared before you settle in and make the space your own. Even a home you have lived in for many years might be hanging onto some dirty laundry like old arguments, sad memories, or otherwise less than cheerful energy pockets. You may get a sense that something is amiss in certain parts of a house, or that people avoid certain areas or rooms, or plants do not thrive in certain places. But many people do not feel auric blueprints and leftovers the same so do not panic if you're not receptive in this way. Space clearing is important whether you know what's hanging around or not.

Thankfully, because we know that energy needs to be transformed, many practices have been developed over the generations to rid the world of such unwanted and unseen influences. We will start first with the practice of the spiritual feather duster.

Smoke Clearing

Smoke clearing for medicinal purposes has been used for centuries, and space clearing using herbs or incense has gained enormous popularity among modern-day pagan practitioners. As with all the exercises in this book, you do not need to call yourself a pagan to benefit from this type of activity. It is a peaceful, simple, and universal way to connect with your surroundings and clear away any lingering negativity binding itself to your home or belongings.

What you'll need:

Many traditions incorporate the use of an eagle feather, but eagle feathers are hard to come by (and illegal to possess), so try another broad and strong feather like turkey or goose.

You will also need some herbs. Native to Southern Europe and the Mediterranean, sage is the plant most often used for these space clearing ceremonies. Meaning "healing plant," sage is burned in bundles and the smoke directed to the areas of the body or space needing cleansing. White sage, sacred to many Indigenous peoples, is under threat of overharvesting so it is recommended that other herbs, like juniper, sweetgrass and cedar, be used for their negativity busting properties.

Finally, you will need some container to hold your sacred herbs, like a heatproof bowl or shell. Some enthusiasts enjoy carrying a burning bundle of their favorite herb around by the hand, directing the smoke where it needs to go. Use precaution when doing either and watch for jumping sparks or falling burned leaves.

How It Works

You will need to flex some of your spiritual muscles for a proper smoke clearing ceremony and really allow yourself to visualize. If you practice paganism or some other religion, you can certainly begin with a prayer to your favorite deity. If not, start by focusing on the energy in your own body before you begin. Your intentions should be clear—aim to remove negativity and replace with new, positive energies. It does not sound that difficult but if you're not practiced at focusing attention in some way, you're going to end up just a person wafting smoke around a room and won't achieve the best results.

Begin with lighting your herbs (windows open!) with a conscious realization of what you intend the smoke to accomplish. Are you banishing an old relationship? A clingy spirit? An argument with a loved one? Even the impact of harsh words can permeate your nest like a bad odor. Focus on what needs to go, then allow the smoke to wash it away. If you just moved in and do not necessarily know what you're casting out, just the idea of deep cleaning should suffice. Visualize the smoke smothering your target with its purifying properties and pushing it out the window. These visualizations are immensely helpful, so try making them unique to you and find one that works. Ants on rotten fruit, fire in a haystack, the Army of the Dead taking down Orcs at Gondor. It's your ceremony, so make it personal and make it powerful.

Smoke clearing can also be used to help clear blockages in the body. With the right intentions, zero in on where there might be areas needing release and break through the chakras and any lingering patterns stunting growth. A well-designed and perfectly planned home won't pack the same punch if you're subconsciously resistant to receiving abundance into your life. Find the black spots in your auric field and clear them out with gusto.

When you're done, dump those ashes into the earth, signaling that they have left your life and have been transformed.

Other Space Clearing Techniques

This should be a no brainer, but clean! Clean your home like you've never cleaned before. If you notice a lag in the household energy, chances are pretty good that a cleaning frenzy might be in order. Wash walls, clean the insides of drawers and cupboards, and use all those amazing tools that came with your vacuum.

It also helps to use nontoxic cleaners. Smearing your home with harmful chemicals kills germs, yes, but also leaves you exposed to a plethora of ingredients counter-productive to the whole *making your home a better place* idea. Go for organic, plant-based cleaning supplies instead.

While you're cleaning up a storm, try flexing more of those visualization muscles again and imagine all of the things being banished from your home in the process. I often use the image of mud to represent the heaviness of negativity and impurity, but there are many other images that work too, and it might take a few tries to find the right fit.

The Broom

Many people like using a broom for this exercise. The broom, or besom, is an old symbol closely tied to witches and other folk traditions. While it was once believed to carry witches to their evening gatherings, the broom symbolizes clearing away physical dirt, as well as illness, evil spirits, and lingering negative vibes.

Have you ever seen a Dyson do that?

If you enjoy the pagan path, are a practicing witch, or just feel like making one of your own, crafting a besom can be a rewarding experience for your space clearing activities. This type of broom is symbolic for the most part, and not ideal for raking up those cracker crumbs under the sofa.

Here is what to do.

EXERCISE
Making a Besom
....

If starting your besom project from scratch, it's time for a good old-fashioned branch hunt. Whether you're magically inclined or not, find the branch that grabs your attention and screams "broom handle!" If you're a random stick enthusiast like me, you probably already have piles of different pieces cleverly organized in a collection as discussed above. I am a huge fan of birch, myself, and will drag home an offcut whenever I see one.

Gather small twigs or some woody herbs for the bristles. If just a ceremonial or symbolic broom, you can add things like feathers and ribbons to make it more personal. If purchasing a ready-made broom, add decorations or your favorite herbs to connect it to you and your home. While crafting your besom, remember to think about how you intend to use it. Your intentions are what creates the magic here, and ultimately the effect of your space clearing efforts.

Start sweeping! Get those visualizations flowing as you swish away stagnant or unpleasant energy around your home. The front door is a great place to start, symbolizing your readiness to usher in the new.

And finally, for maximum space enhancing energy, open the gates! Okay, well, maybe just the windows, but opening windows and doors to let fresh air in everyday will work magic at blowing away stagnant chi. Even in winter, a few short minutes will invigorate the space and stir up the flat air.

Fresh air fuels a healthy mind and body. Opening the windows wakes up the senses. It lets us feel the wind, hear and smell the rain, and savor the sounds of the birds. If you're not heading outside, this is the next best thing.

Below is a meditation exercise that you can try before or after your space clearing efforts. It is perfectly adaptable, and you do not need to be a practicing *anything* to benefit from these sorts of things, so play with it and make it your own. Once you feel you have renewed and restored your perfect abode, you're ready to start choosing what new energetic patterns will take over.

EXERCISE
Space-Clearing Meditation

As with other meditation exercises, this one is entirely personal and should be catered to your beliefs, aspirations, and current level of interest in how energy affects your world. You will do no harm by skipping this section, but you may overlook some important connections between yourself and your space that are fundamental for long-lasting serenity and growth.

Start by standing in the space you want to clear. Look around, noticing the way it feels at that moment, regardless of whether you know its past. Now, find an image to hang onto of something to clear the walls. It could be a paint roller, a giant sponge, a hose. You're going to do some simple pretending here, just like when you were a kid. Imagine washing the walls in your mind, removing everything old and outworn from its surface. You can also do this while washing the walls, visualizing the thorough removal of the stuff clinging to your home. Never downplay the effects of these visualizations. It's pure physics. What your mind believes about your personal space will alter how it functions and that is that.

Now, if there is a window or door in this space—open it. Send out the old energies with purpose, intention, and determination. The last thing you want is to have someone else's spiritual baggage, or perhaps even your own, twisting around your current hopes and dreams.

Get rid of it.

Use whatever imagery you can think of that really captures the essence of making stuff disappear and soon after, you will get an unexpected feeling of renewed clarity and lightness that inevitably comes when something has been cleared energetically.

In that feeling of lightness, start infusing your own aspirations for the space. Feel the warmth of familial love, the stillness of feeling safe, the joy of being comfortable and nurtured. Let these feelings pour out and permeate the walls, the floors, the door, and ask the universe to send only loving experiences into your new home. If you have a mantra, use it. Make this space an extension of what you hope to create in your life, and you will draw it in.

CHAPTER FOUR

Style
How to Capture the Perfect Mood

....

If our homes are the physical extension of our deepest selves, then we need to find creative ways of revealing that in meaningful, harmonious ways.

Before you tackle the exhilarating task of re-wiring your home to suit you, or wiring it from the ground up, it can be helpful to find a foundation that is going to nurture you the most. Some people dive headfirst without a plan of action, and this is completely fine. As creative beings, we often come to form our best creations by accident, so do not let plans and preconceived notions stifle that rudimentary spark if that is the way you operate. Sometimes spontaneity is the very best approach.

Many others, though, see one solitary image grace before them and there's the *aha!* moment that ignites the next four months of solid shopping frenzy. For me, I get it broken down into three simple schematics: color, texture, and overall vibe. If you see an irresistible connection between rustic wood, charcoal grays, and sheepskin rugs, go forth and spend merrily. My new living room sprung up with the sudden image of those three elements dancing in harmony and the result was perfection, but there were also a few unexpected elements that popped up along the way that worked themselves in effortlessly. Always leave room for the unexpected, or a surprise find on your travels (like a pouf. Always buy the pouf.)

Whether planning your style from scratch or not, what you end up with will inevitably fall under some already fortified umbrella of design. Most of us are drawn into or repelled by the energetic patterns of each type.

When I was twelve, I did one of those exercises designed to reveal past life connections based upon architectural styles that I found in a magazine. Probably not the most scientifically proven method of self-discovery, but I was fascinated to learn how much I disliked desert settings and architecture, sixties mod furniture, and fluffy Victorian exaggeration. This exercise works well for clients as well, and sorting piles of images from magazines is a time-tested way to discover recurring trends, patterns, and areas of special interest in a seemingly effortless way.

The point of finding your style is to capture the essence of what energies are likely to serve you on your path from the vantage point of your current self. Just like home types, these common styles carry different elements and vibrations that will impact the way you live and thrive. Here are some popular design traditions and the core elements that make up their energetic foundations.

Rustic

The term "rustic" is broad (and very popular), and often gets itself tossed around to describe many different styles. Maybe you've heard of modern rustic, or rustic modern, rustic farmhouse, American rustic farmhouse, or even rustic contemporary and thought *wow—does every design trend have a "rustic" page hiding somewhere?*

Many of them do, it seems, but some very specific elements lie at the heart of essential rustic design that pave the foundation for the earthy, grounded, and simple pleasures of this way of decorating.

Natural materials dominate here and will energize your life on a very primal level. Wood, stone, metal, and earthly textiles like burlap, linen, and furs will grace a rustic home whether in the mountains or tucked away amid the bustle of suburbia.

Rustic design can be incorporated anywhere with the right use of reclaimed and oversized furniture, cozy blankets, and pillows, and maybe even some low laying ceiling beams overhead. The key to this style is the feeling of comfort. Go for chairs and sofas you can fall into while reflecting upon the simple life by the warmth of a roaring fire. Many rustic styled homes also incorporate elements of traditional design with heavier fabrics and large furniture pieces.

If you're gravitating toward a rustic-inspired home, you may be longing for some serious rest. Indulge yourself and get cozy, even if you live in a high-rise apartment. A rustic home imbues the sense of re-connecting with nature. Think deep forests graced with deer, rocky mountainsides, or wide-open country.

Mountain homes offer great inspiration for a rustic design styled home. Many incorporate strong wood elements, paired with large stone fireplaces, scattered sheepskin rugs and patterned textures on pillows and throws. Searching for ski chalet interiors will also give you a nudge in the right direction. If you can create the feeling of being in the mountains, you're halfway there already!

Traditional

Drawing influence from the eighteenth and nineteenth centuries, traditional design style is made to celebrate, well, tradition! While incorporating much of the warm and natural color tones of rustic design, traditional style is much more orderly and consistent in its execution.

The key here is symmetry and the calm expression of strength as well as timelessness. There is also a distinct flare of color with these styled homes, and deep reds, golds, greens, and blues are often strewn throughout walls, curtains, paintings, and other everyday textiles.

Many people find the energy of a traditional styled home to be stuffy, overbearing, and predictable. While it is true that symmetry is a foundation of this design trend, there is tremendous room here to showcase different cultural influences, textiles, patterns, and rich color schemes.

Traditional furniture is often heavy and enduring but usually more ornate than that of rustic style homes. Wealthy patrons of the past flaunted their positions with finely carved pieces and collections of art and tapestries. Expect a traditional home to exude the same appreciation for splendor as those of older generations, and ornate books will likely be displayed floor to ceiling, paired with antiques or groups of family photos.

Fabrics play a key role in this style, and will adorn windows, beds, chairs, and floors all the same. Many of these fabrics will be patterned, creating beautiful contrasts between varying shades and textiles.

If this is your style, you probably have a great appreciation for history, culture, art, and a passion for civilizations passed. You might be a collector of pottery, statues, or paintings, and perhaps adore the sculptural details of a finely carved crown molding or spiral staircase. This design style offers a rich connection to the foundations of humanity and reveals a deep and enduring interest in the finer things of the world.

Country/Farmhouse Style

If you've ever woken up at dawn in a country home, you know the feeling that accompanies this charming, peaceful, and simple way of life. You will have probably also developed some new opinions about roosters at five in the morning.

Country design style invites a sense of natural peace and reflects, at its heart, longevity and a return to a simpler way of life. Interiors are best characterized by wood, brick, and stone, with wood being the hallmark of this style. Everything from ceiling beams, floors, barn doors, and even wood paneling on the walls reveals the deep connection to the wood element, inside and out. Without the strong foundational energy of wood, it would be almost impossible to achieve the powerful, yet soothing atmosphere of country living.

The color palette often displays soft pastels with the odd touch of bright hues here and there adding hints of personality. A definitive vintage flare also characterizes a country home, accentuating timeless pieces from the past—maybe passed down from previous generations. Make sure furniture in your country-styled home is mismatched, too, as if you personally inherited each piece one by one with care—and perhaps a good story to go alongside it.

Avoid things that look new if working to achieve an authentic country/farmhouse vibe and go for natural fabrics like linen and even sheepskin or cowhide. Faux options add just as much depth, however, and can easily add warmth to that perfect chair beside the fire.

The country home is foundational and is designed for function and the everyday tasks of living a country life. Pantries are organized and stocked with baking supplies. Utensils and pots are always within reach if not displayed on countertops. Rooms always stay comfortable for whoever stops by for an afternoon cup of tea.

Everything in a country home has a purpose. Make sure you are not filling space with items meant to be looked at rather than being used in everyday life. Shelves should be lined with books, magazines, pottery and baskets meant to be accessed regularly and enjoyed often. This style is not meant to impress but rather show off a deep love of the material comforts earth has to offer.

Modern country style is a simpler adaptation of traditional country. It pares down some of those classic bright colors with a more muted palette, more inclined to display that white pottery collection rather than heavy florals and dark green walls. Modern country also enjoys mixing in contemporary lines with the classic comfort and simplicity of traditional country style with a slight hint of minimalism. You do not need to overdo this look, rather go for neutral tones, wooden accents, and minimal knick knacks.

French country design, a popular choice for several years, is a regional adaptation to country style and comes from the relaxed rolling hills of Provence. While France is known for its elegant design, extravagant lighting, tapestries, and gilded finishes, the French country tradition tones down the opulence and blends with it the more subdued nature of life in rural settings.

Here you will still find classic elements of French decor, such as curved lines, finely crafted furniture and ornamentation, but heavy woods and stone elements add a sense of warmth, comfort, and leisure. Pattern is a must here as well and combinations of checks, stripes and toile fabrics enhance the bright cheerful settings of French country homes.

If any of these adaptations of country style is on your decorating radar, you might just be in need of a simple escape from an overstimulating modern world. You may be wondering why you wasted years in the city and are ready for the slower pace of life offered so freely here. You could also have a family history with country life and value the sense of peace and security of raising a family of your own outside the noisy city walls.

Scandinavian

The term "Scandi" design is one of the most talked about and replicated trends going today. Used often by my favorite Scottish designers, Colin McAllister and Justin Ryan, it is "an aesthetic birthed in the Nordic lands of Denmark, Sweden, Norway Finland and Iceland during the early twentieth century by creatives in pursuit of simplicity and functionality."[3]

Minimalism is a core component in classic Scandinavian design, but sacrifices nothing in the way of style, comfort and beauty. Among the elements to look for in Scandi decorating are soft colors like white, tan, or dusty pinks and gray blues with pops of black and lots of wood tones. Mustard yellows and velvety textures play a big role too and invite extra warmth into the homes of those seeking a refuge during the long cold winter months of the north.

You will also see cozy fabrics like that in rustic styled homes, with a particular favor toward chunky knits, sheepskin rugs and faux fur pillows and blankets. Perhaps this is why the trend has become a global obsession, for its ability to capture seamless perfection using the simplest ingredients. If less is more, then Scandi design has it pegged.

Closely attached to the Scandi style is another area that combines great design with a spiritually refreshing way of life: hygge.

Not quite a formal interior design style, hygge's impact on design and interior decorating is so great it deserves a giant shout out. One of Pinterest's most celebrated topics, *hygge* (hoo-gah) is one of my favorite ways of creating a spiritually optimal and nurturing home. Not only does this Danish "feeling" and lifestyle sum up much of this book's philosophy, but it also highlights the importance of allowing yourself to enjoy simplicity for its own sake.

Hygge happens when your world feels right, comfortable, and peaceful—even if only for a fleeting moment. Enjoying your favorite

....

3. Colin McAllister and Justin Ryan, *Escapology: Modern Cabins, Cottages and Retreats* (Vancouver: Figure.1 Publishing, 2020), 11.

tea beside a crackling fire on a snowy night with no place else to be, curling up with a favorite book or magazine, or sharing a home-cooked meal with your loved ones. Moments like these define hygge, but there are many ways to invite this energy into your home every day.

As a design style, hygge shares a few similarities with other trends like boho, rustic, and country. It is at its foundation a striving for coziness, and one that envelops from the outside in. Much like rustic or mountain living, to attain the intimacy and contentment that hygge *is,* your personal space should invite peace, stillness, and indulgence in life's simplest pleasures.

Surroundings should be neutral and reflect the natural world. Stone, wood, and organic fabrics like wool, linen, sheepskin, and cotton are often incorporated, as well as furniture pieces that are comfortable, allowing for maximum relaxation.

Small details are important to create the feeling of hygge. Think warm, soft and plush throw pillows and blankets, cushy carpets for cold feet to land on, and places to put up your feet. Poufs and ottomans are wonderful additions for a cozy lair, and tables close by for a pot of fresh coffee or a bottle of your favorite wine.

Decorating your home in the hygge fashion shouldn't be rushed, though, and what you choose for your space should bring you a personal sense of joy and meaning. Avoid the urge to run out and spend a ton of money on pricey new things for your hygge room makeover. Part of the intimacy of this Danish tradition is enjoying the comforts you have and the small things you celebrate privately every day.

Surround yourself with the things that have become a part of your experience and offer a sense of well-being. These are the objects you want to express who you are, where you have been and what you believe about your part in this lifetime.

The Danes are huge fans of two other things that make up any space inviting a hygge way of life: books and candles. Denmark uses more candles than any other country in Europe, and the burning of candles is the most important part of the Danish way of life. In the long, cold winters, candlelight sparks comfort and warmth within the soul and is considered the most important aspect of creating the atmosphere of hygge. If you're looking for a way to turn any home into a restorative and soulful place to thrive, this is one design pathway to try on your journey.

Boho

Attributed to the wandering Romani peoples of Europe in the nineteenth century, the term "Bohemian" usually refers to someone who is socially unconventional, free spirited, and involved in the world of the arts. It became a label given to anyone living against the norm, and later became the expression of the hippies of the 1960s.

Bohemian design reflects a nomadic lifestyle filled with treasures picked up along the way. Inspired by the Romani people's travels through Spain, Africa, Morocco, Turkey, and France, boho decor boasts a love of world culture different from that of traditional design. Where traditional design typically collects pieces of fine art and sculpture with great historical meaning and academic value, the boho collector is more interested in the unstifled artistic expression of living in tune with the natural, creative world. Independent artists and local artisans speak volumes to those embracing this style, as does anything made for the pure love of unfiltered artistic involvement.

Boho design today has many guises. It might be bright and colorful in one home, white and relaxed in another, or even dark and mysterious. For me, boho style reflects the moods of the artistic spirit—always changing and trying to seek out inspiration. There are some elements, though, that appear in every Bohemian styled home or room that set the foundation for the exciting energy it seeks to impart.

First of all, there is strong visual interest in the boho style, but nothing that requires too much effort to pull together. Bright colors pop from subdued neutral backgrounds like flowers exploding from a garden, and oftentimes jewel tones will sparkle alongside mirrors and metallic surfaces. There is a sense of indulgence here; not one that comes from a desire for material things, but one that arises from a deep appreciation for the simple beauty of an effortless way of life.

Botanicals are rich in boho design also and reflect a love of nature and respect for the environment. Many of the elements in a boho styled space will be organic, like woven fabrics, dyed linens, patterned pillows, and distressed woods. Earthy textures are harmonious with splashes of reds, purples, and blues. Often scattered with sheepskin carpets or life-sized paintings, this style is truly unique and offers a brilliant look into the simple motivations of those who use it.

Seating will be close to the floor in boho design, and pillows and poufs will be scattered around to offer comfort to anyone passing through. Its goal is a relaxed spirit and a space that invites everything. There are no formal rules to this style, of course, and if you're planning the "perfect" boho room you're not going to get far. This is one of those trends that relies heavily on that dose of spontaneity coupled with a soulful guiding in the right direction.

This is one of the most spiritually minded and intuitive design choices and will appeal to those seeking to live life in new and nonconformist ways. You do not have to be a hippie, writer, painter, or tinkerer to enjoy the boho style, but if this is the design path you are drawn to walk down you probably enjoy doing things your own way on your own time. Perhaps it is a time in your life to step outside boundaries, test new waters, and let your hair down for a while.

Modern

Influenced heavily by German and Scandinavian architecture and style, modern design is all about simplicity. Its focus is on removing unnecessary details, such as decorative moldings, carvings, and heavy patterns and giving more emphasis to spatial planning. Emerging and popular between the 1940s and 1980s, it is a trend that has endured into the present and continues to dominate contemporary interiors and building design under new names and branches.

The trend of mid-century modern still captivates today's design industry and is well grounded as the American adaptation to German modernism, particularly the Bauhaus movement. Its key principles of design are simplicity and functionality.

At its heart, modern strives for practicality, and everything in a modern styled home will have a purpose. It does not reflect quite the same simplicity of its "rustic" counterpart, but carries a more functional, unadorned style that aims for cleaner lines and open spaces over accessory and clutter. Furniture is lighter, sleeker, and often lower than that of other trends and in a very broad sense aims to keep space free and clear as much as possible. In modern design, form tends to follow function. The usefulness of the space is at the forefront and there is not much that gets in the way of a modern room fulfilling its purpose.

You won't find many knickknacks in a modern styled home, and even if you do, they will be sparse and cleanly kept out of the way. The robust and romantic embellishments of traditional design will be unheard of here and heavy columns and draperies non-existent. Many windows in a modern styled home are left bare, in fact, enhancing the sense of openness that it is rooted in.

A modern home may also reflect several artistic movements. Many people who design in the modern fashion enjoy some form of abstraction and you may just see sculptural pieces sparsely placed around the home.

Modern style seeks an escape from the weight of the material world and a wider, more expansive expression of personal space. If you find yourself drawn to this style, you are likely seeking a separation from things that might otherwise burden your sense of freedom. Perhaps you are seeking an inner solace that refuses to cling to outdated ideas of material wealth. Simplicity and lightness are key elements for shaping this type of home, so embrace the opportunity to open things up and let the room do most of the talking.

Whatever your style might be, or however many combinations come together in your home, the bottom line is always to make sure it feeds some part of your creative expressiveness and gives you an environment that will sustain your personal spark. When you have your favorite style or styles narrowed down, it's time to work your magic, room by room, in pulling it all together.

EXERCISE
Inspire Yourself

Now that you're aware of the most popular decorating and design styles, it's time to find your true design essence. This is my favorite activity I use on my own clients and is the simplest way to uncover recurring themes you maybe did not know were there.

To get yourself started, you will need to gather magazines. Old decorating and gardening magazines in thrift shops are perfect if you're not keen on snipping up a pricey new issue. Look for anything with lots of house and home photos.

When you have some good materials, start by making two piles. In the first pile, you're going to place cut-outs of things that invoke good vibes. If the picture makes you smile, reminds you of something fond from your past, or makes you say *yes, I want that*, add it to the pile. In the other pile, put in the imagery that has zero impact on your mood whatsoever. If you pass a page quickly without any thought or make any type of funny face when looking at it, add that to the "rejection" pile.

This may sound like something you did in elementary school, because it is! And the reason it works is because our subconscious brain responds well to visual cues, making this simple exercise perfect for finding those connections we make between experience and visual stimuli.

When you have your piles, make a list of any recurring items, colors, architectural features, themes, locations, and textures. Notice obvious patterns, like ocean views, shag carpets, vases full of flowers etc. and start seeking connections to your personal experiences. Sometimes it's relatively easy to connect the dots, but other times there seems to be no discernible explanation for the sudden attachment to colors or other material things.

Use this as a starting point for space planning, putting design emphasis onto those things that filled up your visual wish list. This can also be a good exercise for kids as well, so try it out whenever you're considering any room makeover.

The Physics of Personal Space
What Science Has to Say About Your Sanctuary

....

What kind of car are you? Which African safari animal captures your true essence? What mythological kingdom are you really from? The internet is full of these fun little quizzes designed to fill you in on important details about yourself you cannot believe you did not already know. And while it may not be as important to know if you're a spry woodland elf or a half-ton jeep, it *is* beneficial to be aware of some key energies that drive our creative focus.

When it comes to transforming your home into a place that fully expresses the real you, placing yourself into a category might be a helpful way to begin. Are you traditional? Modern? Country French? Completely clueless? Finding the underlying influence of what you find harmonious will go a long way in steering any home redecorating project and creating a haven to meet your spiritual and emotional needs. We will explore each design style a bit later, but first a look at the science behind how we respond to our personal environments, and how our choices in decor alter, stimulate, or supress wellness. I will show you how to use that wisdom to create a winning combination of inner peace, good design, and personality.

Designers, space planners, and marketing corporations alike know many things about the human brain and have been trained to zero in on what drives our behavior. Being aware of how things like color, aroma, texture, landscape, and art impact our responses has been a fundamental area of study for decades, with the results being manipulated in almost every industry in every possible way.

Restaurants, for example, design and decorate with colors that stimulate the appetite. Hotels will often choose colors that calm, or excite, depending on the location, and will choose surroundings that either induce comfort while away from home or create a sense of adventure (think Disney World). Have you ever been to a themed hotel? These perfectly planned spaces are great examples of how our immediate surroundings alter our experience as emotional beings, so let's explore this area first.

Atmosphere

Atmosphere might be described as a specific tone, effect, or influence. It is the direction our homes flow toward, or the prevailing aesthetic that dominates a space. It is one of the first questions I pose to clients, whether during a kitchen remodel or an interior sprucing up and sets the entire direction for every project. One of my most memorable clients had a heartfelt desire to feel like she was living in the English countryside. Luckily, she did already live on a few acres so transforming her outdoor space was relatively easy. Flower beds went in, old benches laid about, and ivy was trained to climb an old potting shed nearby. Inside, however, was a careful and thoughtful redirection from "flea market chic" to a simple country charm. The difference was undeniable, and what was a house full of old British collectibles had turned into a serene cottage-like bungalow that created the precise atmosphere she was looking for.

When we start these interior projects its crucial to remember that our home is the direct expression of our psyche. It is what we are choosing to believe in, and what we perceive about the world around us. The buildings we construct, design, and fill with personal touch become something of their own and continue to influence people for years—even generations.

Not only does this perspective serve as good practice, but it is also a science. Neuroarchitecture is a fascinating new branch of study into how the brain and body behave in buildings. Eve Edelstein, director of the Human Experience (Hx) Lab at global architecture and design firm Perkins and Will, says "our brain's senses, perceptions, thoughts, emotions and actions respond to the air we breathe, the quality of light, the intensity of sound and the color, texture and dimension of all places."[4]

This signals the importance of atmosphere when designing your perfect spiritually optimal home. If you could choose one place in the world to spend the rest of your days, where would it be? Why? Is it trees you thrive on, or a sandy beach with rolling waves? Do you feel relaxed in city centers, or at peace whenever you visit the local farms?

As an emotional being, you will gravitate to the things that make you feel complete, meaningful, or to whatever makes you feel "at home," even if, on the surface, it seems contrary to your daily life. Everyone has memories, from this life or perhaps other lifetimes, that draw us to settings of familiarity. We resonate with that which lines up with our experiences, whether we are conscious of it or not.

....

4. Amanda Pollard, " How to Design a Home That Boosts Well-Being," Houzz, last updated November 7, 2020, https://www.houzz.com/magazine/how -to-design-a-home-that-boosts-well-being-stsetivw-vs~128031623.

These are your cues, as a spiritual being, to how you should live your best life—surrounded by what truly brings you joy. If you get a hunch to work with a certain color palette or furniture design, it might be worth exploring. But many people ignore these perpetual nudges from the spiritual brain in favor of choosing the most convenient, least expensive, and practical. Some of your whims, perhaps, might be out of reach financially or otherwise, but there are easy ways to create the atmosphere in your home that connects you to your center and draw upon the energies you desire in more practical ways. The key here is to acknowledge them and find small outlets to let them in.

Back to my deer pictures. I own several, as well as many things faux fur to add to that mountain cabin feel. But there are many other things that go into creating a specific atmosphere, and color is among the most explored, celebrated, and useful.

Color

Color is one of those things so closely entwined with human experience that most of us are unaware of just how deeply it works in our daily life. Many of our daily decisions, in fact, involve color, from the clothes we buy to the food we eat to how we judge other people. We analyze the color of our food and its corresponding nutritional value, the impact of a red shirt versus a blue shirt for a job interview, or the stereotypical attributes of a person that drives a shiny orange SUV over a subdued silver sedan.

The study of how color affects human psychology has been a hot topic for years, especially within interior design, art, and marketing. Color has also played a part in many healing traditions. In ancient Egyptian myths, the art of chromotherapy (using colors to heal), was discovered by the god Thoth. Both the Egyptians and Greeks made use of colored stones and crystals, as well as minerals and dyes, as remedies for ailing patients and even painted their "treatment sanctuaries" in various shades of colors.[5]

But while every culture accepts the important role color has on the mind and body, not everyone shares the same response to color, making the practice of color therapy a very individual process when looking to re-design a home suited best for you. Below is a list of colors and what they might mean in your design choices. While they won't be the same for everybody, there are some common beliefs about what these colors do for the soul, and how you may be able to use them to your home-enhancing advantage.

Red

Perhaps the most vital of all colors, red touches upon something truly invigorating within us. Red is primal. Red is survival. It is the color resonating with your base chakra and serves to ground you to all things instinctual. Red was one of the first colors used by prehistoric artists who would grind down red ocher to paint on cave walls as well as their bodies. The ancient Egyptians also used red ocher as a rouge and lip color and even in today's cosmetics, the same pigments are often used to bold and daring effect.[6]

In China, red is auspicious and is both the national color and the most popular one. To the Chinese, red represents good fortune, happiness and success and is a prominently used color for attracting fame in the application of feng shui.[7]

....

5. Helen Graham, *Discover Colour Therapy* (Berkeley, CA: Ulysses Press, 1998), 5.
6. Anna Pokorska, "Colors of Ancient Egypt: Red," London's Global University Blogs, last updated December 4, 2018, https://blogs.ucl.ac.uk /researchers-in-museums/2018/12/04/colours-of-ancient-egypt-red/.
7. Fercility Jiang, "Lucky Colors in China," China Highlights, last updated December 1, 2021, https://www.chinahighlights.com/travelguide/culture /lucky-numbers-and-colors-in-chinese-culture.htm.

Varying shades of red, such as cinnabar (a mineral) and vermilion (a pigment) were also prized highly throughout ancient Rome. Red was used in ritual and ceremony and continued in popularity in all art forms throughout the Renaissance.[8]

From a psychological and physiological point of view, red seems to invigorate the nervous system. It is the color of blood, and thus our entire inner workings on the physical level. It stimulates strong emotions and is usually linked with passion, anger, appetite, and aggression.

Wearing red can increase feelings of confidence and dominance, triggering an instinct to out-perform and conquer. This may stem from a natural evolutionary response to red as carrying a stronger life force, greater vitality, and overall advantage over others. Wearing red might make you perform better, so the implications for home design are encouraging when we need to rally some triumphant energies for goal attainment.

In a more spiritual light, red activates the base, or root, chakra. If you're not up to date on your chakra stuff, this is located at the base of your spine and is where you keep your connection to your physicality and earthly life. This chakra governs your primal, animal nature and your will to survive. Wearing red, designing with red, or working with red crystals or minerals is believed to help heal blockages in this chakra and re-align your connection to the earth plane.

This is not a color to go crazy with in your design plans, of course, due to its natural potency and ability to rile things up but is definitely one to boost your life force if you're perpetually off to a slow start. Reds are better used in accent pieces, to draw and entice you in rather than smack you in the face with overstimulation. Red

....

8. The Conservation Center, "Pigment of the Month: Vermillion," last updated August 28, 2019, http://www.theconservationcenter.com /articles/2019/8/28/pigment-of-the-month-vermilion.

ignites the senses and too much red will be counter-productive to the home you're hoping will sustain your spiritual equilibrium.

A red accent wall is great but soften the fire with some earth tones and avoid going for overkill. Pillows, rugs, throw blankets or lampshades are all simple ways to bring in the elevating energy of red without overwhelming the space. Softer shades of red, such as pinks, can be used for a definitively feminine look and are also nice touches when striving for a romantic feel.

Orange

Orange is exciting! It's bold. It's zingy. It's one of those colors that truly invigorates with its zest for life and boldness of spirit. I drive an SUV with the color name "tangerine comet." Seeing my car in a parking lot amid a sea of silver and white makes me happy because it stands out like a lonely flower in a field of wheat.

Orange is often thought to be the happiest color, and it does not take science to find out why. But, if we want to look at the science, orange often makes people happy because of its seemingly inherent ability to uplift and energize on a psychological level. Born from bright and vibrant yellow and passionate red, orange is the color child of adventure and can make us feel invigorated and inspired. Orange is a bright sunset, a refreshing slice of citrus, an exotic tiger, the warmth, and comfort of autumn and the turning of the seasons. It is the burning flame and the reassurance of the harvest.

Orange is also the color of the sacral chakra, which sits directly above the root chakra at the pelvis. This chakra is connected to our passion for life, and our ability to experience sensuality in our worlds. It is also the color most associated with high levels of activity and off the beaten path adventures.

The robes worn by Buddhist monks are traditionally orange, and the use of saffron or turmeric powder are usually used as dyes.[9] Orange, it would appear, was also a favorite color of Vincent Van Gogh and looking at his *Willows at Sunset* is clear testament to the amazing power of orange to capture the vibrancy of a setting sun.

When using orange in your design and interior decorating plans, the same rules apply as with other bold colors—less is always more. Orange does not need much room to impress or impart its awesomeness and can be tricky to get right. Stick to softer shades of orange for furniture, or a few smaller accents to let this lively spectrum of shades pop like fireworks.

Use orange in social rooms, or anywhere people are likely to gather for good food and conversation, or a home office to get those creative juices revved up to maximum.

Yellow

While an energizing color, yellow has a more complex set of associations in our culture and a very curious past. Yellow pigment has been admired since prehistoric times. Indian Yellow was a favorite pigment among many prominent Medieval and Renaissance painters (including Van Gogh) despite being obtained from the urine of malnourished cows, fed only mango leaves to intensify color. Eventually outlawed, Van Gogh's *Starry Night* was one of the last paintings ever made with the Indian Yellow pigment.[10]

Today, the boldness of yellow is used for eye-catching marketing and street signs and is often used as a color alerting danger. In color

....

9. Jessica Stewart, "The History of the Colour Orange: From Tomb Paintings to Modern Day Jumpsuits," My Modern Met, Last updated February 21, 2019, https://mymodernmet.com/history-color-orange.

10. Kelly Grovier, "The Murky History of the Colour Yellow," BBC, last updated September 6, 2018, https://www.bbc.com/culture/article/20180906-did-animal-cruelty-create-indian-yellow.

psychology, yellow has been shown to increase metabolism, raise energy levels, and boost mood, but it can also cause feelings of frustration. Yellow is the hardest color on the eyes due to its brightness and has been shown to increase tension in people surrounded by too much of its more abrasive tones.

But, on the plus side of the yellow coin, it does spark feelings of happiness in many people and generally represents an upbeat, optimistic outlook on life. It is said to stimulate the intellect and spur on new ideas and creative solutions.

The third chakra, the solar plexus, is represented by yellow and governs our clear thinking, intellect, personal power, and charisma. Our ability to laugh and express our true joy with confidence lies within this color.

In the interior design world, yellow can be used to great effect when seeking a charismatic boost to a dreary room. If you're going to decorate with yellow, choose your tones wisely and use the experiment at the end of this section. Because of its intensity, you might want to see how much you can tolerate before slapping those lemon tones on the kitchen walls. Many rooms with dominant grays, whites or blues do well with an accent piece, like a yellow chair, but if you plan to paint the walls in the yellow spectrum aim for soft and pleasing variations. Think butter tones or pale golds instead of sharp glaring shades.

Green

Said to be one of the most restful colors for the eyes, green is an important backdrop to life on earth. Much of nature is green, of course, and instills a deep appreciation for the beauty of the planet. Rich, organic, raw and powerful, green is a foundational color and is associated with healing in many cultures. The Egyptians saw green as the color of new life and regeneration and would grind down malachite, an opaque, green-banded mineral, for their pigments.[11] The hieroglyph for *green*, in fact, was a papyrus stem and frond.

Green is the lush grass of summer, the fullness of the forest, and the health and fertility of a new shoot sprouting from the dirt. It is the color of youth, the signal to move forward, and the resonating vibe of good health.

Author Mary Webb once said: "Green is the fresh emblem of well-founded hopes. In blue the spirit can wander, but in green it can rest."[12] There is a gentle balance in this color capable of both uplifting and restoring.

Green is the color representing the fourth chakra, which is the region of the heart. This chakra is where we learn to live from a place of love for others and develop a strong love of self. A connection to nature has always been important for feeling the interconnectedness of life and so green is the emblem of atonement with our creative source.

In some pagan traditions, like modern-day spell craft, green is the color associated with money, prosperity, and the acquisition of wealth and it's not uncommon to see the use of green candles in money spells.

Although green is seen everywhere we look outside, it is often overlooked as a design color for interior spaces. Aside from creating green space with plants and trees, using green to paint walls makes for a soft, peaceful and unique room when paired with other down to earth colors.

Many shades of green work well in bathrooms and bedrooms, such as sage or mint green, and often pair in decorating schemes

. . . .

11. J Hill, "Colour: Green," Ancient Egypt Online, last updated 2010, https://ancientegyptonline.co.uk/colourgreen/2010.

12. Mary Webb, *The Spring of Joy: A Little Book of Healing*, (London and Toronto: J.M Dent and Sons Ltd., New York: E.P Dutton and Co., 1917)

with white and wood accents for a "spa" type feel. Green is the color of healing, after all, and can work magic in this application for a peaceful space. Many homes following the country style framework incorporate greens, mimicking the lush outdoor landscape of rolling country hills or open farmland.

Blue

Blue is a color deeply entrenched in our culture and has one of the most fascinating histories among humanity, largely because it was one of last colors to be recognized. There is a curious lack of the blue pigment in the natural world, and the first society to have a word for blue was the Egyptians—the only culture able to produce blue dyes.[13] When Egyptian blue hit the market, it soon became one of the most prized possessions in the ancient world.

Many flowers and birds that are blue do not actually produce the blue pigment but simply create it either through biological processes or through the reflection of light.[14] The visual perception of blue has always been a treat and it's no surprise that blue is often chosen as a favorite color among children and grown-ups alike. Every shade of blue carries a soothing, introspective, even a brooding kind of energy capable of both commanding attention and cooling emotional fire. Blue is the color of the free and limitless sky, the vastness of the seas, and triggers on a psychological level the search for peace and tranquility.

....

13. Fiona MacDonald, "There's Evidence Humans Didn't Actually See Blue Until Modern Times,"Science Alert, last updated April 7, 2018, https://www.sciencealert.com/humans-didn-t-see-the-colour-blue-until-modern-times-evidence-science.

14. Andy Lowe, "Why is the color blue so rare in nature?" The University of Adelaide, last updated August 20, 2019, https://sciences.adelaide.edu.au/news/list/2019/08/20/why-is-the-colour-blue-so-rare-in-nature.

In contrast to red, blue is perceived as a "cool" color and is icy, placid, and reserved. Blue is inspiring, but in a way that creates a conservative, reliable approach. It also has a decidedly pacifying effect on the nervous system and creates a profound relaxation in both mind and body.

On a spiritual note, the fifth and sixth chakras are both shades of blue. The throat chakra is blue and speaks to us about our ability to express ourselves through speech. This is where you learn to speak your personal and spiritual truth and communicate your needs openly. The brow chakra is a radiant indigo, which is technically halfway between purple and blue on the color spectrum and governs the third eye. This is where your psychic abilities are housed, as well as imagination and the ability to perceive other levels of reality.

In design, blue is a dynamic color to fuse into your home and an exciting tool to work with. Using blue in the home is a wonderful way to invite some much-needed serenity and has that magical ability to fulfill many different design ideas. Darker shades of blue can add some bold formality to a room, complementing shades of white, gold, and most wood tones. Pale blues make restful choices for bedrooms, family rooms, and nurseries by adding that soothing aura of a clear sky. Try adding yellows, whites, and pale green tones for a classy, timeless, and carefree feel.

Purple

Not many things in nature are colored purple, much like blue, which makes this a truly unique and intriguing decorating choice. Although violet is on the color spectrum, purple is actually a combination of red and blue and often receives a mixture of interpretations as to how it makes people feel. I love the color personally, but the one time I used it to paint my bedroom walls I discovered how much it stirred my subconscious. I could not sleep for almost two weeks, had the most vivid dreams of my life, and eventually gave in and replaced the deep purple with a pale lilac. But do not let this deter you. Everyone responds to color in different ways, and sometimes this too can change throughout a lifetime.

Many have claimed that purple or violet is a spiritual color and represents the crown chakra at the top of the head. This chakra is the source for inspiration and spiritual guidance (which may explain the overactive dreaming brain), and among color therapists, chakra specialists, and others with healing backgrounds, purple is a color of divine connection, spiritual ideals, wisdom, and power.

A color of wealth, royalty and prestige, purple was reserved for those of high rank and riches in the ancient world. First produced by the Phoenicians, Tyrian purple could only be derived from the mucous of sea snails along the coast of the Mediterranean.[15] To have the kind of moola needed to acquire so many you were either an emperor or a king and duly entitled to pillage the seas without care. It was even illegal to wear purple if not the king and doing so would have gotten you killed. It could have taken thousands of sea snails to produce just one strip of purple on a toga, and the fact that the species behind all of this great high-end fashion, the *Murex Brandaris*, did not go extinct in the ancient world is mind blowing if one considers the wealth of the Roman empire alone.

Thankfully, synthetic purple dye was discovered in 1856 by Chemist William Henry Perkin,[16] by accident, allowing purple to be used more abundantly by the masses and thus sparing the helpless sea snails from being wiped out completely.

....

15. Jacob Olesen, "The Rarest and Most Expensive Colors in the World Throughout History," Color Meanings, last updated 2021, www.color-meanings.com /rare-expensive-colors-world-history/ 2021.

16. Science History Institute, "William Henry Perkin," last updated December 14, 2017, www.sciencehistory.org/historical-profile/william-henry-perkin.

Decorating with shades of purple is sure to add a sense of luxury to your home. Not a color to be overdone, however, as a little purple always goes a long way in design schematics. Paint a purple feature wall for a little drama and class or indulge in purple bedding for a rich and exotic aura and get to know how you respond to this complex color before making the same mistake I did.

White

White rarely needs an introduction, and still stands at the forefront of many design and interior decorating trends. While many see an endless opportunity for stains, others see a crisp, pure and infinitely untouchable entity from which to build their fortress of solitude.

In the west, white has always been adored for its seemingly etheric quality, imparting feelings of lightness, space, purity and cleanliness. White is associated with angels, otherworldliness, innocence, and peace. It is equality, fairness, and the perfect balance of positive and negative forces. White represents a fresh start, a clean slate, and overall good health while enhancing a sense of lasting peace. It provides the ambitions to declutter and create space in our homes, our lives and our spirits.

But as with every color, white has complex meanings across the globe. White in many Eastern countries symbolizes death and mourning and is often the color worn at funerals.[17] It also represents metal in feng shui, and can be seen as a sterile, cold, and indifferent shade. Too much white, as seen in hospitals for example, can impart a starkness that is neither pleasant nor inviting.

When using white in your home design, tune into how white makes you feel on a subconscious level. White can make things

....

17. Carrie Cousins, "Colour and Cultural Design Considerations," Colours & Materials, last updated November 7, 2014, https://coloursandmaterials .wordpress.com/2014/11/07/colour-and-cultural-design-considerations/.

infinitely bright to look at and amplify feelings of space. Overdone, however, like in the classic all-white kitchen design, it can leave a room hanging in a monotone nightmare.

Many people are still drawn to the all-white trend, of course, for its timeless and neutral appeal, but in the design industry I see more shifting toward an organic way of expressing colors, even in kitchen design, which places white harmoniously alongside wood and earth tones. A little color goes a long way to compliment that clean, fresh look white offers while grounding it in something more substantial.

Black

Not most people's first choice when decorating, black is one of the most complex shades you can utilize in home design. Not really a color, black is made up of all of the light waves in the visible spectrum. Black absorbs light, making it a mysterious entity in human cultural history. Here in the West, black often harbors connotations of sadness, depression and spiritual burdens and is what we typically wear to funerals. Across much of Europe, Asia, and North America the association between black and mourning has remained for centuries and continues to be viewed as a portent of influences deemed evil or otherwise unpleasant. Even black cats are considered to be the carriers of evil spirits, and many people still believe in their ability to bring about bad luck. In Africa, black takes on a slightly different meaning, representing maturity, masculinity, and age.[18]

Black also reflects an air of mystery, depth, darkness, and allure. Like a croaking raven, the color black invites into the psyche things beyond the lighter shades of life. From blackness comes everything, and it tends to carry a heavier vibration than other colors and has

....

18. Bernadine Racoma, "Color Symbolism—Psychology Across Cultures," Day Translations Blog, last updated July 26, 2019, www.daytranslations.com /blog/color-psychology/.

become multicultural representation for black magic, the black arts, and the mysterious beyond.

But black in the design and fashion universe hints at something far more sophisticated. It is a strong and protective shade and is usually seen as a symbol of class and wealth. Tuxedos are black and represent a refinement of style, formality, and status, as do most black cars and black dresses.

In architecture, black has become a dominant choice for exteriors, providing a powerful statement of longevity and structure. Whether burned wood or sleek black metal, black grounds everything around it in a subtle, effortless endeavor.

When it comes to interiors, however, black should be used very carefully. Black in the house tends to darken a room so ensure you compliment your black with the appropriate levels of light. A black feature wall is a nice touch for an elegant or rustic styled room, chalk walls are a fun way to use such a deep and serious color. Paired with wood or some eye-popping whites, you're sure to make a statement.

When incorporating black into a space, zero in on the overall look you're hoping to create. Black is a powerhouse of energy and does not work in all applications, but with the right design and implementation black can heighten a room's aesthetic and add some extraordinary depth and character. Under the right circumstances it can even have a meditative vibe, inducing sleep and relaxation. In feng shui, it is the color of water so can be used to represent this peaceful element to great effect.

Before making those final decisions on palette, try this exercise to see what directions to take your visual cues from.

EXERCISE
Color Meditation Exercise

Now that you know everyone reacts to color differently depending on experience, taste, and resonance, I recommend trying this exercise with the color spectrum before solidifying any bold color decisions for your home. Despite reading all of the traditional color meanings and associations, you might be one of those people who views things a little differently.

You can do this meditation anywhere, and whenever you come across a color that jumps out at you. You can also sit quietly at home with a color wheel, or paint swatches you nabbed from home reno stores, and begin your silent color quest.

Once you have a color in hand, look deeply at it. Do not stare if it bothers you but close your eyes periodically and then resume visual contact. It's also helpful to look at varying shades of the same color to notice any inclinations or aversions that may come with severity and saturation.

After a few moments, you will start to notice things jumping to mind about what the color reminds you of, and perhaps some memories popping up along with them. Notice the feelings you're getting, the thoughts, the ideas, and pay attention to how your body is responding. Many people find instant aversions to certain colors during this exercise while others enjoy spending some time with each hue.

This exercise is not just about picking the right colors to make a room look good, but more about trying to understand what we resonate with on a deeper level and designing our homes in the direction of more subtle cues. Sure, taupe looks good on the walls and goes with just about everything but is it a color that might bore you in six months, or does it remind you of a sandy beach, your favorite latte on a cold winter morning, or the color of your childhood dog? These are the little things that get tucked away unnoticed during our busy daily lives and are the exact details we should be acknowledging in our quest for a home that serves our highest potential as spiritual and emotional beings.

When you finished this meditation with your select colors, or all colors, keep a notebook of all the key ideas, words, or sensations you gathered. You may want to go back and try this again years down the road and see if anything has changed. Experience fuels our relationships to all things, and you might be surprised how you bend and sway as the years pass.

Scent

Although not the basis in most home design plans, the utilization of scent in your remodeling scheme can have an amazing impact on the overall vibe of your home. Its ability to influence well-being is well documented, researched, and celebrated and can be well utilized to complete or enhance any room in the house. When working to design a home to soothe the soul, the exploration and use of aromas can be a powerful tool on your journey.

We are captivated by smell right from birth, using this sense to learn about our world. The smells around us shape memories and inevitably become a part of our connection to our culture. The foods we grow up with, our mother's perfume, the smell of a fresh cut spruce tree during the holidays. We keep these aromatic links tucked away in our memory banks all through life, to the point where one solitary whiff can send us back decades in time.

Smell is linked to those parts of the brain that process emotion, making this sense an exciting frontier in behavioral science as well as marketing.[19] This scientific knowledge has armed the perfume industry with some very potent marketing power, using a multitude of sensory cues to get us hooked on fragrance.

When creating your personal sanctuary, take your time to learn what scents trigger what feelings, moods, or reflections. An old client of mine had a peculiar attachment to lavender. Not only did she grow it, but she also baked with it, made lavender-scented pillows, and ensured that no part of her home was devoid of the smell of it somewhere. There are less intense ways to incorporate aromatherapy into your home, of course. Try adding some natural essential oils, fresh aromatic flowers, or cut cedar logs for some amazing natural ambience. This last one in particular is an excellent addition to a rustic or country inspired home. If you can trigger some peaceful, joy filled memories by using the right aromas your spiritually optimized home will be off to a soaring start.

Sound

Nobody can deny the power of sound and what it does to our mood, and what your home sounds like can have major influence over your well-being. If you're like me, silence is bliss, but so are the restful noises of nature.

Thunderstorms, the wind rustling through the trees, owls chanting their magic spells through the night. All these sounds create a connection to nature that eases the mind and invigorates the spirit. City living often poses a whole new set of sound challenges, and if you're sensitive to noise disruption, aim for a residence with calmer surroundings if possible.

....

19. Sarah Dowdey, "*How Smell Works*," How Stuff Works, last updated October 29, 2007, https://health.howstuffworks.com/mental-health/human-nature /perception/smell.htm.

When I have noisy neighbors, I have a hard time enjoying things. But while you cannot always control the chaos that goes on with other people, you can create a calm oasis *inside* your home for those times you need a noise break. To block unwanted sounds from the outside, there are a few tricks you can try, like keeping a fan handy to thwart noise, using a sound machine, or plugging in a water feature temporarily for a peaceful escape.

To create a calm and nurturing audio experience on a regular basis, try opening the windows on a breezy day. Not only will the sound of the wind invigorate you, but chances are also good you will hear the creaking and rustling of tree branches and leaves or the faint jingling of a nearby windchime. These are highly meditative activities and immediately bring focus to the present moment no matter how far your mind may have wandered. Keeping windows open, even for short periods of time, also invites the day-to-day sounds of the birds singing and croaking, or the rain tapping down.

Another way to call upon a rejuvenating sound experience indoors is to play music. Having your favorite playlist going while doing chores or relaxing with a cup of tea is a sure-fire way to heighten the mood. Choose music that makes you cheerful, conjures up good memories, or invites a quiet reflective moment. Every life has a soundtrack, and we all resonate to our own individual rhythms and beats. Find yours and let the sounds of your life permeate your homestead.

Lighting

Not many people would contest the importance of light, for it is the medium by which we are able to see our world. It sounds so simple, yet often people downplay or neglect the subtle effects of light in their own homes. There are so many elements of a healthy organic life that depend on light, though, that it is one of the most important considerations in interior design you will read about everywhere.

Through its properties, light creates specific conditions which can influence our perception of just about everything. Lighting design is the deliberate planning of our visual environment and a crucial component to making sure our homes are optimized for overall health. The right choices in lighting not only affect the way you feel but will determine the overall benefits of other elements in your home like how colors look, how textures appear, and how big or small your interpretation of a room is. Light is a pivotal element in home design, and its impact on mood, well-being and energy are second to none.

When planning your rooms for visual optimization, nothing compares to natural light. Whether you're blessed with large windows or not, open heavy curtains and blinds during the day and let the outside filter itself in. This daily connectivity will keep you grounded and remind you that there is a big wide wonderful world outside your human constructed abode.

Perhaps you can remember a time you had a bad flu and were bedridden for a day or two. Maybe you could not get out of bed to open the drapes, and maybe you watched TV for hours on end. Many new parents experience this postpartum, when night and day blur together and the normal cycles of life become enmeshed with the needs of a newborn. When you do get back to normalcy, the difference is enthralling, and you often feel as though you were stuck in a dream. The appearance of the sun is a testament to the continuation of life each day and has always been celebrated throughout human civilization.

A spiritually optimal home keeps you connected to the world around you, and light is a powerful force in that equation. Because lighting is, of course, necessary indoors, choose location and brightness carefully, ensuring comfortable levels of task lighting, overhead lighting, and ambience lighting. They should balance out for a natural effect and create a sense of calm. Candles and fireplaces are great for a soft glow and create a soothing balance to artificial lamps when enjoying a quiet evening. Dimmer lighting should be used during times of relaxation, such as before bed, to help ease the mind and prepare for sleep.

Brighter lights tend to keep you alert and awake so bring in plenty of natural and task lighting to a home office setting, kitchen, or anywhere you plan on getting to work and getting things done.

The Green Stuff

I have decided to add a discussion of plant life here because of the inexhaustible energetic boost you can get from a few well cared for houseplants. These incredible living things release oxygen during the day, helping keep the air fresh and suck in some not-so-nice toxins floating around your home.

The incorporation of plants in the home is not just a neat design trend, nor a simple luxury. There is a whole school of architecture that studies the crucial importance of green space in design called *Biophilic Design,* analyzing the way we can once again fuse our concrete jungles with the necessity of being immersed in nature. Until recently, much of our architecture has served to distance and alienate from the natural environment. The entire premise of biophilia is that we all have an innate love of and need for nature. Without it, we suffer, even when we do not realize we are suffering from its absence.

By adding plant life into every room in the home, or building our homes around the natural world, we can bring back a primal balance lost in today's bustling urban lifestyle. Trends like boho, rustic and country are already infused with natural elements, but the biophilic movement steps that up to the next level. A tree might be seen growing in the middle of a home where the building was crafted around it, or a river, perhaps even a waterfall, could be softly flowing adjacent to an open plan kitchen. The main idea is to some-how experience nature indoors, and not to separate ourselves from its empowering aesthetic as soon as we close the front door.

Melding this trailblazing new design trend into an existing home is just as beneficial as working with an architect on a new build. Your scale may be smaller, but the impacts and dynamic energies of let-ting the outdoors inside will be monumental to your health and spir-itual connectivity.

And you can start in very small ways, like picking a species of plant to study, care for, and grow indoors. Plants like succulents, snake plants, and orchids release fresh oxygen day and night, even when no photosynthesis is happening, and they make wonderful green friends for beginners. They also assist in nurturing a good night's sleep if kept in the bedroom and are always a joy to see bend-ing toward the morning light when you first wake up.

Feng shui enthusiasts and practitioners will caution heavily about placing plants in the bedroom due to their very strong moving yang energy, but because home design is a very personal and spiritual journey, test the proverbial waters here and play around with the possibility. When it comes to creating greenspace indoors, go with whatever gives you a sense of peace and nourishment. Design trends and philosophies are guideposts, meant to be tried, challenged, and made personal.

From a spiritual vantage point, you will reap the benefits of reg-ular houseplant care from their connection to the earth element. Watching things grow and thrive under your watchful eye is a tre-mendous way to strengthen that bond with nature and enhance your intuition. You will start to get a sense of what your plants need, and this is a great practice you can spill over into the rest of your life with your own needs as well as those of others.

From a design standpoint, plants offer not only physical beauty but are also fantastic for adding depth, height, and visual interest wherever there is empty space. Taller plants can act like pillars, framing a room, window or extra space left over behind sofas and chairs. Choose plants that fit in with the light you have available. If large tropicals appeal to you, make sure you can offer them the light and humidity they need to thrive. If you are designing a room with a particular theme in mind, try adding plants that blend in with your style. Many country homes are filled with flowering plants, while succulents are often found scattered amid desert and Boho decor.

No matter what plants you choose, your air will thank you. You will also find your spirits uplifted and restored instantaneously. There are times, though, when live plants do not suit a home or lifestyle. Perhaps you travel a lot, have pets that chew everything they can find (many plants are toxic to pets when ingested), or maybe you have allergies that prevent you from gathering flowers indoors. If any of these apply in your particular case, you can still enjoy the visual beauty of plant life in many other ways. Try adding some landscape artwork for that touch of green, or silk plants to liven up a room. Just seeing imagery of plant life or a lush garden can have a profound effect on your daily moods.

There are many things that go into crafting a perfect home and I encourage you to experiment in all of the above. Have fun with it and take your time finding the right combination for you.

CHAPTER SIX

The Entry

How to Let the World in Through Your Front Door

....

When you first visit a building, you may be aware of just how dedicated your attention becomes to first impressions. It's as if layers of analytical processes creep to the surface and work to decipher some very key elements about the building's existence: is it safe? Is it clean? Do I want to step inside, or stay there?

You might be completely mindful of this energetic assault or not, but it happens everywhere you go. From restaurants to boutique shops downtown to a new friend's home, your psyche makes instant decisions about the places you go and your likelihood to want to return in the future. Knowing this sort of thing is a good start when crafting or re-crafting your new intuitive home and should focus your enthusiasm on a powerful entrance. What you do here will set the framework for everything that tramples across your threshold.

Whether you call this amazing and magical space a foyer, entrance hall, reception area, vestibule, or mud room, historically this was once the most important room in the home. It is that magical place that stands between the outside world and the personal little universe you have lovingly created.

The foyer is, interestingly, largely believed to have gained its domestic importance in ancient Rome. To the Romans, the clear separation between public space and private space was spiritually paramount. The home was sacred, being guarded by the family's patron gods and goddesses and required clear boundaries from public view. The door to a family household was like a veil, dividing the inner workings of family life from the harshness and uncertainty of the world outside.

Janus was worshipped throughout ancient Rome as the god of gateways, passages, and transitions, expanding our modern perspective around the way we have celebrated this crucial space over time and in our homes today. If the front door was sacred enough in the past to have its own gods, then the very least you can do is to make sure your entry space is clean, in good repair, and free from dormancy.

But it wasn't just Rome to adopt this high standard for the front doorway. In the ancient Chinese practice of feng shui, the front door is called the "mouth of qi" because, it is believed, the entry is how energy and life force enter the entire home. It is often called one of the most important spaces in the house and should be carefully tended to ensure you are ushering in the right vibrations for a happy, healthy home.

Chinese folk religions also paid special attention to the threshold guardians (called *menshen*) of gates and doorways, and even made sacrifices to door spirits. These door gods were believed to stave off evil and encourage positive energy into the home.

To the Japanese, the entryway is a place to leave the outside world behind, much like in ancient Rome. Japanese ancient and modern architecture incorporates a designated entry called a *genkan*—the floor of which is normally sunken to sit lower than the main floor for guests and occupants to remove footwear before entering. This separation prohibits dirt being tracked inside. In smaller abodes where floors cannot be so situated, a separate tile or other flooring surface clearly marks the location of the genkan and its space within the home. This is a prime example of how we already use certain symbolic elements to clearly mark our spaces to affect our psychological and spiritual aspirations.

Throughout modern history, the function of the "hall" retained some regal glory in large palaces, where guests were greeted and swept into the wealth and austerity of their hosts. But sadly, as life withdrew deeper into larger family homes the hall lost its original purpose and became more of an entrance lobby with a staircase, or a room to be received in and pass through on the way to more important spaces.[20] Many homes today pay little attention to this magical space, leaving it the family's place to throw shoes and drop sporting gear after a game.

No matter who you plan on inviting inside your front door, be it the queen or the cable guy, incorporate some good design into your new home, or start a love affair with your existing entry space, playing with its unique, untapped potential to express the tone of your household's energy. In short, it's a good place to show your company what you're all about!

You will find endless images of front entryway ideas on your visual search, no doubt, and while many seem beyond the normal scope of ordinary homes. But if you look closely, you will notice similar themes and applications that will work in every space. Some of the common elements of good entry design are *perspective*,

....

20. Bill Bryson, *At Home: A Short History of Private Life* (New York: Doubleday, 2010), 77.

simplicity, and *comfort*. Good design is a science and is about manipulating the energetic patterns all around us.

Follow the tips and tricks below to make the most of your foyer, and lock in some of that old-fashioned magic harnessed by the ancients.

The Great Divide

Now that you know your front door is really a magic portal, you might want to make sure you have the space clearly marked just in case you forget. Most front doors on single-family houses have steps, or a wooden front porch, or at least a concrete path leading to the front of the home wedged between a lawn or little flower garden. Many of us are good at figuring out our way to a front door because of this obvious design standard that lures us onward to the next great step of the adventure: the front door.

From the outside, the basic architecture of every home has a distinct boundary, like the ones of ancient Rome, signaling the point where public life ends and private life begins. After reading this book, you will likely start noticing these "boundaries" wherever you go and see the tell-tale signs of where this division is meant to begin. Some larger homes, or estates, start this separation at a gate that leads to a driveway passing lawns or gardens or water fountains, all leading toward the front of the home. There may be statues guiding the way, or lights to seduce your arrival. But no matter how grand or humble a home is, the marker is clearly set, and this is the threshold where the world stops, and your little universe can begin.

Many designs play on this idea of the portal, or threshold, as if ingrained into our spiritual brains, by adding personal guardians on either side of the doorway. They may be pillars, lion statues, potted trees, or Greek gods statues, but nevertheless it is a signal to the subconscious that something is going to change the moment we pass through. And indeed, it does.

Keeping the front entrance clean and clear is crucial for ensuring positive vibes can find you. Before you even put focus to the inside of the door, make sure you have your outdoor threshold in good repair and in good design. Steps should be strong and sturdy, with nothing loose, crumbling or absent for the obvious reasons of injury. Gardens and lawns should be tended regularly, and dead flowers and weeds pulled seasonally. All of us know the value of curb appeal, and this is really your first impression. Not everyone will step inside your sanctuary so use this outdoor space to show off your design savvy, or at least showcase your love of beauty and harmony and respect for your individual piece of paradise. Changing the outside decor of your home seasonally will give some extra oomph to that ever-flowing chi working to find its way to your direction and delight those people who walk past your house every day.

You can also maintain this clean-cut separation of space upon first entering the home by using the Japanese genkan discussed previously. If you are building a new home, or renovating an older home, you can add in a sunken area for a designated place to remove footwear, outerwear, and to symbolically leave behind the outside world. Many of the things we do each day revolve around unconscious rituals meant to fulfill some daily need. Making the front entryway an obvious place to enter the private world you have created is a fantastic way to leave certain things behind—like work, busy traffic, bustling neighborhood streets or bad weather. If you do not have the option to make a physical separation or sunken floor, try using a different type of flooring upon entry, or even a large door mat.

No matter how you choose to divide your interior from the outside world, do so with good intention and try visualizing what you would like to see stop at the door. Remember to imagine, too, what you hope to let in when working on this energetic undertaking and weave those thoughts into the design as you go.

Mirrors

Often called the aspirin of feng shui, mirrors have always been considered magical, enchanting, special objects throughout history. Used for centuries by those in the magical arts, mirrors are said to be like portals to other worlds, with abilities to attract whatever they reflect. The first mirrors used by humankind were polished stones like obsidian, with polished copper being used much later. Glass was first being used for mirrors during the third century CE, but with the advent of glass blowing the convex mirrors we know today became increasingly popular.

Mirrors are full of superstitions all over the world and have always been tied to the idea of the soul. Many believed that a mirror could trap a person's soul, and when a person died their mirror might have been covered up to keep the soul from escaping.

In the dynamic universe of interiors, mirrors, and other reflective objects are like secret weapons for good design. The wonders they bestow upon *any* space make them must haves for not just the entryway, but any space devoid of spatial abundance. Mirrors reflect light and give the immediate impression of much larger and brighter space. Hanging a mirror where it reflects a window is an ideal placement, especially in the entryway, creating the appearance of more interior space and flow of light. It amplifies the expansiveness and freedom of the outdoors and the beauty of the natural world. Be careful not to place a mirror directly across from the front door, however, as many design and feng shui practitioners believe this reflects back all that new, fresh energy trying to come in.

It is also believed that mirrors double or multiply whatever it is they reflect, so choose placement with care and amplify things that represent warmth, comfort, and good health. For an entryway, this is especially important because you are using this space to draw in the things you want your home aligned with. Try not to let a full-length mirror reflect piles of shoes or unhung coats heaped beside the door—multiplying a mess might make a bigger mess from the perspective of mirror magic.

In apartments or condo applications, the use of mirrors can be the saving grace of that cramped energy at the front door. Do not be afraid to use large mirrors in small spaces either; mirrors create the illusion of depth and will make even the smallest entryway expand its architectural limitations. A good, practical use of mirrors in any housing style will go a long way to transforming a nonexistent transition space into one that welcomes fresh new energy every day.

Seating

When decorating your entryway, nothing says *welcome* like a nice comfy chair (or if you're clever, a mat that says *welcome*). If room permits, seating at the entryway can serve multiple purposes. For starters, it allows you and your guests a place to sit comfortably to remove or put on footwear without doing the balance-on-one-foot routine. This instills an immediate sense of comfort, ease, and a thoughtfulness that cares about whether you might fall over. That kind of feeling will linger well into the rest of the house and as a guest, a deep sense of hospitality will already be blossoming.

In homes where the front door leads right into the living room, seating can be a great way to break up the quick energy trying to rush you inside. Having not clearly defined "welcome area" can feel like a push too quickly into the heart of the home.

Correct use of seating is also a perfect solution for larger foyers, especially ones that are long and/or adjacent to a staircase. In my home, the front door opens into a long hall that faces the stairs directly. Because this is considered a feng shui "no-no," I decided to use a bench to divide the space, providing both a place to sit, and breaking up the energy from the main door up the stairs. According to the experts, the restless energy of stairs (with the constant up and down movement) causes chi to rush up and down without dispersing throughout the home properly.

Stairs at the front door should have some grounding element to slow down all that incoming chi.

But seating does not have to be overdone, of course, and most of your guests will not be expecting a baroque high-back chair to be awaiting their arrival. Even a single wooden chair beside a small apartment door will work wonders. Because this is still your "first impression" room, make the chair or bench something unique and interesting—toss a faux sheepskin rug over the back, or pick a stand-out color that really pops against the backdrop.

Lighting

Because not every entrance is blessed with large windows (or any window) lighting should be another key element in your magical front door design. Light is the strongest manifestation of energy, symbolizing illumination and joy. Light instantly affects our mood and directly impacts feelings of motivation, comfort, and positivity. Not only is good light exposure good feng shui, it's essential for optimal health. It's not hard to see the correlation between a poorly lit home and the productivity of its occupants.

If your entryway is abundant with windows, open up blinds and curtains in the morning to make the most of new energy, and if no natural light source is available, turn on a light for a few hours each day. If your "mouth of qi" is short on space and natural light, a table or console can hold a small lamp. Wall sconces are also optimal if you're trying to keep floor space free and offer a more comforting and balanced light energy than an overpowering ceiling bulb. For extra illumination, remember the clever use of mirrors and how they amplify what they reflect—so let there be light and enough free flowing chi to go around!

Feng Shui for the Entryway

Considered one of the most important places in any home, the entrance is your personal portal into your spiritually optimized space. It is also the first part of the home visitors see upon arriving and will no doubt impact the way others perceive you as well. If you use the implications of the law of attraction in any way, the state of your home is a direct magnet for the types of things you will create. Making the entrance to your home clean, harmonious, and visually pleasing is a great way to start ushering in beauty and abundance into your abode.

Feng shui is very specific about what makes a good, efficient entryway, and some of them were mentioned briefly above. Use the applications below to call in the best chi to your home and keep the flow of good vibes going as you move from room to room.

Use the Front Door

The formal front doorway is an important place for new energy to enter the home. While many people use alternate doors regularly, like the garage or a side entrance, the main front door was designed to be the passageway into which you greet your home upon return, and where your home greets you. It should at least be opened every day if you're not using it as the main way in.

If your front door happens to be facing an "unlucky" direction, using another door might be the more favorable option. Check your bagua for the most optimal location for entry. It is also considered good feng shui to make sure the door is kept in good repair, so if the paint or stain is chipping, give it a makeover.

Clear the Path

Clutter is an energy killer in every room, but clutter at or near the front door is a big problem in feng shui. Keeping your front entrance free of obstacles is symbolic of how you want your life to work. If you're hoping to allow opportunities to find you quickly and effortlessly, you should make sure your entranceway is not overgrown with weeds or last year's dead flowers. Keeping the inside of the door tidy is just as important. Pick up the heaps of shoes and jackets that always seem to find their place on the floor when kids get home, and things like backpacks, mail, umbrellas, or that cool stick someone found on the walk home.

But shoes are always a big one. As we saw in the Japanese tradition of the genkan, taking off the shoes in a separate area marks the leaving behind of the outside world before entering the sanctity of the familial quarters. If you do not have the setup to make a formal separation, at least keep the footwear off the floor and out of sight. When you walk into a home, there should be nothing stopping you from taking the next step inside, and even better if it arouses a feeling of wanting to stay.

Add Definition

Having a front entryway that is also your living room can be tough. I once had the challenge of decorating a small character home that situated the living room and first bedroom right when the front door opened. Not only was the layout small, it was also confusing as a first impression when you walked in. A clearly defined entrance is the best way to welcome, gather and distribute chi as it arrives, so taking the time to make this space look like its own entity will boost the energy and allow you and your guests a proper introduction upon arrival.

If your front door directly faces a staircase, chi might rush up and down too quickly without getting the chance to flourish and flow properly through the space. If you have a large foyer with some architectural detailing, then there is likely enough room for energy to move about before moving on. If you open your front door directly onto a staircase, try adding a feature like a large plant, a piece of artwork, or small piece of furniture to stop the new chi from dissipating too quickly.

Make it Count

Not just good feng shui, but good common sense, a welcoming entrance to your home should be something we all aspire to. Some things in life do not require ancient philosophies to figure out, though, and this should be one of them. You walk into enough buildings every day to notice how they make you feel upon first impression. You react instinctually to a house or business by how it looks from the outside. It's in your nature to judge and categorize the good, healthy, and beautiful from the run down, ugly, and uncared for. Admit it. You do it every day—probably without much thought whatsoever. Make your front entrance worthy of greeting any guest and you will never be embarrassed to answer the door again.

More Expert Tips

Now that your foyer is bright, reflective, and offers a convenient place to sit, there are a few more tricks for keeping the entrance to your home both welcoming and magically enhanced. If we go back to the Romans, the idea of a patron deity speaks to our primal need for a sense of security—even at home. If you walked into my front doorway, you would see Athena, resting yet watchful with a pile of healthy plants nearby. To me, Athena represents guardianship, and her placement holds significance for me in the protection of my family. But this is just me, and depending upon your personal beliefs and practices, you may choose a Buddha to sit at the front door, welcoming peaceful and meditative vibes, or maybe some very intimidating dragon statues to scare away the wrong types of people.

Some homes are donned with feng shui fu dogs (or Imperial guardian lions) to add a sense of protection to the home and are often seen traditionally in front of Imperial or government buildings. They also signify family wealth and social status so definitely worth thinking about for that nicely cleaned up entryway.

Runes are another great way to enhance your entry if you are inclined in the ways of North magic, and who can forget Gandalf carving the rune *Fehu* onto the front door of Bilbo Baggins in *The Hobbit*. If you do not want the trouble of carving symbols into your door, chalk works great too, and small runes can be drawn discreetly anywhere around the entryway—just ensure you have a clear idea of what you want them to attract or repel during their application.

The point of all of this is that whatever you place in your home's main entry point is meaningful to you, and will create a resonance with the experiences you hope to draw in. If it's excitement you crave, use bold colors and lively art. If serenity is what you're after, leave it simple with some fresh flowers and a neutral entry mat. The entry can also be a great place to showcase a favorite group of objects—like curious seashells or a whimsical feather collection. Make it a playful space and allow it to set the tone for a joyful home and new opportunities. Remember, the entryway is the seat of everything that comes through your house and the things you hope to attract. Do not overlook its value in your spiritually optimized new home.

Keep it tidy, keep it bright, and make it count!

Crystals for the Entryway

The general consensus among crystal experts is that black tourmaline is the best crystal to place at the entrance of your home for its powerhouse of protective energies.

Deities for the Entryway

What seems clear from archaeological and anthropological evidence is that our ancestors, dating back thousands of years, prayed to the gods and goddesses, alongside other magical creatures, with great ambition to keep the home safe, blessed and free from the uncertainties of life on Earth. There are, in fact, several house spirits and deities found all over the world who have acted as guardians for both individual families as well as entire cities. Most animistic and polytheistic traditions have some concept of a being who protects and nurtures the household in one form or another, and worship of those beings was most often kept on the home front.

Janus

Worshipped extensively in the ancient Roman world, Janus was the god of doorways, beginnings, and transitions. While not necessarily a hearthside deity, Janus was revered as a protector of the passage between public and private life and was a crucial spiritual presence in the Roman household. The front door marked the very clear separation from the outside bustle of the city and the sanctity of the familial domain along with its peace, comforts and security. One of the oldest gods to be worshipped in Rome, Janus marked the transition from past to future, beginning to end, and ruled over the stepping in and stepping out of the home. Janus was depicted as a god with a double head to reflect this duality of nature.

EXERCISE
Meteditation for Guiding the Right Stuff In

Like the first page of a great story, what you showcase at the front door lets everyone know what kind of adventure they're in for. But to do this, some soul searching might be at hand, particularly if you've never worked this hard to design an entry area before.

As with any meditation exercise, make yourself comfy and clear your mind of the day's busy energies. Cozy pants on, bra off, kids fully occupied or asleep.

This meditation is useful after a good clean and overhaul of your existing entry space. Traditional space clearing rituals, as discussed in the previous chapter, might be helpful too, especially if you are moving into a home recently left by another family.

Start thinking about your front door area. Imagine it like a passageway, a place that bridges the hectic world of work and sports and shopping with the restful abode that welcomes you in after each day. Really allow this idea to emerge until you can sense the importance of the door, as the ancients did, for dividing space and altering experience. Imagine it first as impenetrable, keeping out negativity and danger. If you have a god or goddess or other household deity you work with or are drawn to, ask that being to be the guardian of that doorway and everything that resides behind it.

Now, imagine opening that same door. Feel a rush of cool energy sweeping through, invigorating everything in its path. Imagine it touches the floor, the walls, bounces off a mirror and catapults its way up the stairs or around the next corner. Imagine this energy is carrying pure, raw, and undiluted potential as it moves through your entryway like a playful water spirit. This energy charging its way through the doorway carries whatever you want it to: good health, money, career success, fertility, love. But this energy needs space to move.

When you come out of this meditation, start looking around your blank canvas that is your foyer. You will start to notice the right places to add extra light or hang mirrors. You will feel where the energy is stagnant and what parts are whisking it right through. Take time with this exercise, and really home in on how the front of your home feels to you. After some dedicated work on this special part of your home, you *will* notice how drastically other areas of your life begin to change. I have never not noticed positive changes in my life, or that of others, after a front entrance makeover. Is it magic? Maybe. But it's also the clear intention of letting new and exciting things come your way.

CHAPTER SEVEN
The Kitchen
Nourishing the Body and the Soul

....

More than any other space in the family home, the kitchen has been through the most interesting evolution in our modern design history. What started out among our ancient counterparts as a cauldron boiling over an open fire has turned into a billion-dollar industry with more bells and whistles than even an experienced kitchen designer like myself can keep track of. If your kitchen has a drawer within a drawer within a drawer, you're not alone—and you may also be in *Inception*.

But while the industry caters to the ever-demanding clientele of busy working families with a supersized obsession with cupboard organization and gadgetry, it's still refreshing and exciting to home in on some of the traditional comforts of the kitchen and how they can uplift us every day.

In the beginning, the kitchen was not always the go-to room of the house and was once kept as far away from the rest of the home as possible. Early kitchens caught fire easily, smelled terrible, and were hot and smoky until the widespread use of chimneys in the sixteenth century. The kitchen as we know it today did not take its form until the 1940s, owing mostly to the end of the Second World War and the continual advancements in cooking technology. The built-in kitchen was finally born as the slow shift from stand-alone pieces dispersed in favor of fixed storage, and with the societal gravitation to both make food and entertain in one conveniently stylish location.

Designing a new kitchen, however, can be a long and arduous process—which is why kitchen designers exist. With countless rules and building codes and layouts to choose from, along with the high financial entanglements often involved, making the most of your kitchen will go a long way in helping you nourish yourself and your family for years to come.

Imagine your kitchen as more than just a room to make food. It is *the* place in your home where you cultivate, wash, and prepare ingredients. It is where new recipes are born. It is where we create the food that sustains our earthly bodies and where we savor the daily bounty of the earth's endless harvest. The kitchen can be full of excitement for little ones as well, mixing up the cookie dough for the first time and learning to whisk, roll, and measure.

The kitchen has a life not found in the other rooms of a home and for this reason deserves a special treatment and consideration. Energetically speaking, it is the room that represents our sustenance, prosperity, and ability to sustain wealth. When you start focusing on bringing good vibrations to your humble abode, the kitchen should be at the top of your list.

Here are some common elements of kitchen design and how you can apply them when creating a spiritually enhanced space.

Layout

If you're into your feng shui, you will already be aware of optimal placement for a kitchen. Ideally the kitchen sits at the back of the house, keeping the family's wealth private and energy away from escaping too quickly out the front door. It is an active room, and whether you're building a new home or renovating an older one, layout is key to lasting comfort, efficiency, and good health.

Although its popularity has waned in recent years, some of the best kitchen layouts will have a hint of the "work triangle." This magical triangle (made a kitchen design staple in the 1940s) may not be as potent as a magic circle but offers much in the way of functionality and ease, even eighty years after its original conception. It was a kitchen design standard built around the idea of a single cook, at a time when kitchens were small and appliances big. The golden triangle solved the problem of how to move more easily between the sink, stove, and refrigerator, making food prep time shorter and leaving more time for cocktails.

While still an effective way to design a kitchen, the last few years have seen a surge in "kitchen zones," accommodating more people in the kitchen at once, and ensuring a place for everyone to carry out their individual tasks with ease. If your kitchen space is generous, allowing spaces for food prep and clean up, baking, cooking, or a coffee bar, will invite the flow of cooperative meal planning within the family. It is also often a place to do homework or catch up on work emails, and if there's room for the wine too—even better!

So, what are the rules to live by when designing a new kitchen? While this is not an in-depth book on the subject, a few tips and tricks will make your kitchen experience a whole world more convenient and noticeably more nourishing for body and soul.

Let It Flow

Not everyone uses their kitchen the same way, and when it comes to optimal layout your household's daily routines are just as important to consider as the cabinets you choose. Keep "zones" close together that are likely to be used simultaneously such as the prep counter, a sink, and waste bin. Do you love to entertain guests while you cook? Consider an island if space permits with plenty of seating, and do not forget to keep a bar fridge close by to serve drinks hassle free. The kitchen is a great place for good conversation so anywhere people can gather will add refreshing, vibrant energy to the home.

Let It Breathe

Ensure you invest in good ventilation. Food smells and grease can dull even the brightest and newest kitchens, so match your cooking load to the best hood fan you can find. This will also help in the feng shui department to keep that wholesome energy moving. If an expensive new appliance is not in the budget, consider keeping the window open while cooking to keep the clean air flowing through.

Go All the Way to the Top

Floor to ceiling cabinetry is a great way to maximize space in smaller kitchens. For a galley style kitchen, this could be the design of your dreams, pushing prep and cooking spaces close together while offering up a ton of cabinet storage. If you're short like me, a nice rolling ladder or sturdy stepping stool will help you reach those hidden chocolates at an eight-foot ceiling height.

Move the Fridge

The biggest appliance to contend with, keeping the fridge out of the way of main cooking areas is the best. Many kitchens these days even give the fridge its own wall entirely, casing it in with pantry storage or a bar area. If this is not an option for you, placing the fridge at the end of the cabinet run will free up that working counter space, and if you absolutely do not need the biggest refrigerator money can buy, do not buy it. Sacrificing a few inches on this appliance could mean more counter space or a larger cabinet somewhere.

Keep It Clean

It should go without saying, but keep your countertops cleared when not in use and maintain a healthy routine of cleaning appliances. Your kitchen works hard for you and deserves a little TLC at the end of each day. You should wake up each morning to a kitchen space ready for another busy day without the leftovers of yesterday's casserole to haunt you.

From an energetic point of view, having a kitchen that works with your daily needs is the best you can give yourself. If you're renting and have no control over your kitchen's current layout, or cannot afford a total kitchen overhaul, you can still find peace with the space by maximizing what you have. Find the rhythm and make the space personal for you. I have been designing kitchens for many, many years and I still do not yet have my "dream kitchen." For most of us, working with what we already have is a more likely reality. Add in a movable island if you have room. Upgrade the faucets or cabinet hardware. Organize the drawers and counters to accommodate your daily needs in food prep and cleanup. No matter what type of home or kitchen you currently have, there is always room for improvement and some personal touch.

Materials

The kitchen houses your premiere fire energy in the house according to feng shui and is one of the most complex rooms from an elemental standpoint. It is the only room that uses fire, wood, water, earth, and metal at once daily and should be balanced in its fundamental design. Incorporating the right combination of materials will create harmony and prevent one element from dominating the space.

When starting from scratch, consider what structural elements to incorporate. When working with a pre-existing space, lean heavily on easy remedies to ensure a gentle cooperation of all elemental energies.

Cabinets

Wood is still the best choice for your cabinetry in aesthetic, durability, and energy. Wood feeds all that fire energy and is believed to fuel the good health of its inhabitants. Natural woods are ideal, with alder, maple, cherry, and oak being the most commonly used. Wood makes us feel secure and instills the sense of longevity and generational value. Ensure you keep your wooden cabinets in good shape, repairing any chips and scratches to the finishes. As the room that speaks of your family's health, signs of damage and neglect will have an immediate subconscious impact on your sense of well-being.

Laminates/Thermofoils are a common find in many kitchens, and usually start to wear and tear in about ten years. If these are the cabinets in your kitchen, add some nice wooden accents like heavy wood cutting boards, and an oversized mortar and pestle made of granite to add strong earth energy.

Glass doors in kitchen cabinets are a nice touch and allow for a hint of elegance when showing off some fine stemware and adds some reflective qualities to the space. Consider a feature cabinet, or top row of glass insert cupboards to draw the eye upward.

Countertops

Quartz and granite remain the most popular countertop choices for both beauty and durability. They are powerhouses in the energy department and add heavy grounding earth energy in any application. Nothing dazzles quite like the amazing sparkle of a stone counter, and many granites are sculptures handcrafted by the earth for hundreds of years. Stone adds a richness to the kitchen that speaks volumes on a subconscious level. Like the architecture of ancient times, stone dominates as a sign of wealth and instantly creates a feeling of stability, uniqueness, and abundance.

From a metaphysical perspective, quartz is a stone of power and amplifies intentions, energies, and thoughts. In the kitchen, this will increase the bounty of good nutrition, good health, and overall wellness for you and the family. Granite, being comprised of quartz, likewise adds tremendous healing properties, and enhances the ability to attract abundance into your home. If you can afford the expense of stone, go for it!

Wood tops, mainly bamboo or butcher block, are another good choice for countertops. They carry the natural wood element that fuels the fire of the cooking appliances and are relatively cost effective. If your cabinets are a natural wood stain, however, I would advise against a wood top. Your goal is to balance the elements here, not pick favorites. Wood tops will work best with painted cabinet styles, thermofoil, or high gloss finishes.

Accessories

Whether you like to think so or not, the state of your kitchen can reflect the state of your love of self, and your willingness to care for your physical body. Even if you do not enjoy cooking, keeping your space clean will benefit you no matter how often you use the kitchen.

You do not need an expensive or extravagant kitchen to attract good things either; my favorite kitchens, in fact, are small, natural spaces with practicality and effortless comfort. Here are some ways to add warmth, joy and the brimming feeling of a healthy lifestyle to yours.

Storage is a crucial part of every kitchen, and one of the most time-consuming aspects of kitchen planning. Keeping your appliances, dishes, cookware, and utensils orderly and out of sight creates an optimal flow of positive chi and lets others know the effort you put into a healthy family home. Of course, the kitchen won't *always* be spotless. We might have kids and jobs and maybe a writing career on the side and we do not care about doing dishes at midnight sometimes. But, if everything has a home, like a drawer, a basket, or a place in the pantry, it becomes easier to maintain the ever-bustling room that now houses mealtime prep, homework or homeschooling, and quality family time all at once.

Baskets make great containers for sorting small food items or spices in the cupboards. Clearly labeled and sorted, you can cut the time immensely when searching feverishly for the cinnamon. Use cutlery dividers to organize daily wares and keep knives out of sight. I know many people like to display their mighty chef knives for the world to see, but it can add some harsh and uneasy energy to your kitchen. If you follow feng shui, this is a top of the list no-no.

Cookware comes in many styles and functions, and images of giant pots boiling on the stove harken back generations and hold fond memories of parents and grandparents in the kitchen. Displaying pots and pans is a favorite design feature for many and adds a warm, rustic feel.

Feng shui advises against hanging heavy pots directly over a prep area, though this can be a great space saver for smaller kitchens. Do some visual research for some amazing and creative ways to hang and display your pots such as ladders, tree branches, or old wagon wheels. If you're going to keep anything out on display in your tidy, well-organized kitchen, make it a nice set of shiny copper or stainless-steel pots.

Food is a great way to attract abundance into your home. Keep a large bowl of fresh fruits on the counter to display bounty and good health, and make sure your pantry and refrigerator are stocked with healthy foods that have not gone past their expiry dates. Remember, the idea is to attract more of what we love and want to have more of, so moldy bread at the back of the cupboard and liquid lettuce in the crisper will give off the energy of decay rather than that of fresh new life. Keep your favorite recipes and cookbooks handy too, as they show a love for food and a passion for creating the good life every day.

Recipes for Good Health

The above tips and tricks will help you maintain a happy, healthy home through the good energy cooked up in the kitchen. Because you are working to draw in more efficient energy, try these spells and other "secret ingredients" for being mindful of what you want to bring into your life.

The goddess Abundantia is the deity of prosperity, and the cornucopia is her symbol of the ever-flowing bounty of the universe. Fill a cornucopia or small bowl with ingredients that represent abundance—rice, dried herbs, nuts, seeds, coins, and shells—and place it in your pantry or other food cupboard. This is a powerful way to keep the image of material wealth in your home's aura, and lets the goddess know you are grateful for the blessings you receive each day.

As mentioned above, keeping your kitchen clean and tidy is essential to ensuring the health of you and your family. Keep a good supply of natural, plant-based cleaners handy and clean bins ready for composting and recycling. When you clean off counters before or after food preparations, imagine you're washing away old, stale energies to clear the way for something new. It may have been a great dinner party with lots of good wine and several plates of apples, but clear off those residual leftovers and be ready to start fresh. The same applies when sweeping the floors: do so with the intention of space clearing and you'll notice the freshness in the air and the amplified energy in your kitchen.

Cooking a meal is a magical ritual. Scientific research has already shown that food made with positive intentions tastes better, and likely nourishes those it feeds even better, too. Most of us recognize this on some level, because we are aware that the entirety of existence is composed of energetic patterns working together. But when you ground that awesome knowledge in everyday applications, you can truly transform your life. Take the extra time to wash and care for the food you prepare. If you grow some of your own food, you're already a rockstar and probably operating on super wavelengths of nutritional joy. When making meals for yourself, for family or even friends, pour into those meals not only your gratitude for the abundance at hand, but for having the people around you to share it with. Your everyday meals will start to take on incredible spiritual significance when you take the time to notice just how blessed we are to share in this earth's wholesome and nourishing supply.

Feng Shui for the Kitchen

With all the elements going on in the kitchen, it is one of the top three rooms to pay attention to in feng shui along with the bedroom and the front entrance. This is your most feisty fire element room and represents your family's health and abundance so you're going to want to keep this space in tip top shape as much as possible. There are rules also of creating and maintaining a feng shui friendly kitchen; some are structural and can only be done correctly in a new-build or renovation setting, but many of them you can attain with a pre-existing kitchen.

Placement

Sadly, unless you are building your home from the ground up the location of the kitchen in your home will be frustratingly beyond your control. According to experts, the kitchen should never be in the center of a house or at the very front—because that is asking for trouble. The kitchen is considered the heart of the home, so having your home's "heart" on fire is thought to bring bad fortune and health problems for the family. Alternatively, a kitchen at the front of the house keeps the family's symbolic wealth too close to public view and could jeopardize the security of assets. A kitchen at the back of the house is ideal. It is also considered a big no-no to have the kitchen close to a bathroom, so if you're space planning for a new build, keep the toilets as far away as possible. if you already have this problem, keep the bathroom door always closed.

Layout

As a kitchen designer, I know how long planning a kitchen reno can take, but according to feng shui there are some very simple rules to follow to optimize the harmonious interactions between the elements, especially fire and water, and keep things functional. The first rule states that the stove and the sink should never face each other or be too close in proximity if running along the same wall. Granted that many small kitchens or galley style kitchens will run into this issue no matter what, if you're able to avoid this keep these two work centers as far apart as possible while still maintaining an effective work triangle.

In feng shui, the stove represents your resources in life and opportunities for success and wealth. Choose a stove with multiple burners to increase your chances for abundance and ensure you can see the door when cooking to maintain a command position and have a view of who is coming in. Keeping your stove and oven clean is also important if you're to be ready for new and exciting things, and it also ensures good health while preparing nourishing meals for yourself and family.

Some extra tips for a good feng shui kitchen: Because the kitchen is a primary fire element room, make sure to add some wood in there to fuel it. Even a few cutting boards or fresh herbs growing on the windowsill will do.

Keep the fridge clean and free of old or expired food. Doing a deep clean regularly ensures you are only feeding your family the very best and symbolizes your expectations for the ongoing abundance of the earth. Do not let the fresh flow of resources get backed up with rotten fruits or moldy cheese.

As mentioned above, keep knives off the counter. Many people enjoy flaunting their chef knives for all to see, but on a subconscious level most of us are leery about the potential dangers of such sharp objects. From a feng shui point of view, it's better to keep the knives tucked away when not in use to avoid unintentional feelings of uneasiness.

Keep appliances and kitchen utensils in good working shape to gain the most beneficial energy out of the kitchen. This goes for dishware too, and anything with chips or cracks should either be repaired or tossed.

Crystals for the Kitchen

Carnelian is said to add a boost of fire energy in the kitchen and inspire creativity for the chef. Clear quartz also offers purity and is excellent when preparing nourishing meals for the family.

Deities for the Kitchen

Lares and Penates: Guardian deities of ancient Roman religious life, the Lares were beings who stood watch over the boundaries of their domains. Passed down from the earlier Etruscan family and ancestor cults, these protective beings were, it seems, deified spirits of deceased relatives who ensured the longevity of the family line. Ancestral spirits were linked to the Lares, while more domestic spirits were linked to the Penates, who were the "spirits of the cupboards" who helped with the maintenance of the Roman house and who were vital to the sustenance of life.[21]

The Lares inhabited every public and private space. Each traditional home in ancient Rome had a Lare and housed an image of their personal house lord in a shrine along with other important deities or ancestors. Lares also occupied public places, and there were Lares that guarded cities, agricultural lands, seaways, and even the military.

Alongside the Lares were the Penates, or "pantry gods," ensuring the family's wealth and prosperity and protecting the stocks and supplies to keep the family healthy and well fed. Over time, the Penates merged into the guardianship of the whole house with the Lares and formed a trio of familial household protection and assurance of abundance and lineage. At state level, the Penates helped keep citizens—parts of the larger, communal family—loyal and protected under political change and social unrest.

....

21. Susan Stewart, "Reading a Drawer," *Room One Thousand*, 2 (2014): 14–30, https://escholarship.org/uc/item/4t87g8bw.

EXERCISE
The Cornucopia
....

One of my favorite exercises for the kitchen is the filling of the cornucopia. Even if you're not inclined for ritual, this is a fun way to get the idea of abundance going and if you have kids, have them join in. While often an activity for the fall season, representing the harvest, you can do this anytime of year, or several times a year with the changing of the seasons.

First, get your vessel. You can buy a pre-made cornucopia from most craft stores during autumn, but any container will work fine. Some people like to use a cauldron, a favorite bowl, or even a wooden box or basket.

Next, gather some supplies that are both easy to preserve and are representative of overflowing supply. Things like grains of rice, dried corn on the cob, seeds, coins, fake fruit, and dried flowers are all good visuals of the bounty of the earth. As you, or your children, fill your chosen vessel, imagine how things poor easily into your daily life and how the vessel replenishes itself effortlessly. This is a crucial exercise because many people struggle with feelings of lack, separation, and not having enough, and granted there are times when we all face financial challenges, this simple gesture can remove mental barriers that might prevent good things from reaching us. There is something magical that happens when we start trusting the universe to fill our proverbial bowls with goodness.

When you have finished, place your vessel someplace safe and know you will always be provided for.

The Bedrooms
Magical Places to Dream and Restore

....

Most of us grown-ups find great sanctuary in our "master" bedrooms, and those of you who do not, really should. Aside from flower arranging and moving furniture around, one of my favorite childhood pastimes was gazing dreamily at the well-made beds in the Sears catalog. I wasn't a very exciting child, but oh boy did I love those layers of pillows and perfectly tossed throw blankets!

In many design traditions and philosophies, including feng shui, the bedroom is one of the most important rooms in the home. The bedroom is a place to rest, rejuvenate, meditate, and dream. It is the most personal space you inhabit, and if you can only focus on one room to redesign or organize to get started, let it be this one. If you really think about how many hours a day and night you spend here, it's not hard to realize the importance of the energy swirling around and how it will be impacting your well-being.

But tackling such a spiritually crucial room can be daunting and should be considered with care. Swimming within the endless ocean that is interior design we have choices like never before, from mattress material and bed frame construction to duvets and pillow shams. It can be hard to decide what bedroom will bring you the greatest peace and restoration, but when you do find the right fit, you will find immense comfort in the sanctuary you create for yourself.

Beds

Beds today promise luxuries never seen hundreds of years ago. In Victorian and medieval times, the best material for a bed was feathers, which required regular fluffing and turning for optimal comfort. These mattresses filled with heavy down sat on lattices of ropes, tightened with a key when they began to droop. This is where the expression "sleep tight" comes from.[22]

But the luxury of having a feather bed in those days meant the continual attraction of rats, moths and bugs which just loved the smell of old feathers. Servants would be required to empty and air out these mattresses periodically to keep it fresh, and usually freshly plucked goose feathers would be added.

If you were not particularly wealthy, however, you would have slept on piles of straw, where you would be required to "hit the hay" each night to scare off bugs that had settled inside. Thankfully, you have some better mattress choices ahead of you than the folks of the past. Your bed will be the most important element of your newly fashioned sleeping space and is considered the most important piece of furniture you will ever buy. Spend some time getting to know your options, your tastes, your budget, and your actual workable space. If your largest bedroom is scant on floorspace, a four-poster bed might not be a reasonable choice. Make sure you leave room for walking space and perhaps a place to sit. A room with just an

....
22. Bryson, *At Home: A Short History of Private Life*, 379.

oversized bed might not give you the feeling of a luxurious place of restoration. On the flipside, if you have one of those bedrooms that could double as a small apartment, splurge a little on something to dominate the space, like a bed frame with some character or height.

In the tradition of feng shui, the best material for your bed is wood, providing a sturdy foundation for a healthy night's sleep. Wood represents the expansive element of growth, and fuels the energy of fire, your passions, and your heart. Wooden headboards can be classic and traditional, or modern and light. They offer a myriad of styles and energies and are highly adaptable to changing decor and color schemes.

Upholstered headboards have always been popular and offer both security and the element of softness. These types of headboards are great for the soft and sophisticated look and add an aura of relaxed elegance to any room.

Metal is often frowned upon for the bed in feng shui due to its cold, impersonal energy. If you're designing within the parameters of this design tradition, steer clear of metal bed frames if you can, or at least refer to the feng shui "cures" for this elemental addition.

The benefit of having a metal bed, though, is their cost effectiveness compared to wood and upholstered beds, but keep in mind the tendency of these types to mimic things like cages, gates, and even jail cells. The open spaces on these frames may reduce your sense of security as well, but as with any design style, use your own sense of comfort and choose what feels right for you and your space. No amount of design advice, from books or professionals, will outweigh your own sense of personal taste. Always design from the soul and shop from the heart. Try adding extra pillows to a metal bed frame, faux fur throws, or those extra poufy comforters that billow over the sides. The warmth of a few well-chosen accents can tone down the colder vibes of the metal element.

No matter which bed you choose, make the dressings comfortable and personal for you. Do not buy fabrics that itch or cause overheating during the night. Do some research into which materials might be best and invest in some good quality sheets. Egyptian cotton is great in the warmer months, allowing the body to breathe during sleep, and cozy flannel is a super treat over winter when body heat needs to be trapped under those blankets for optimal comfort.

The same rules apply to pillows and if you're going for the perfect sleep experience, make sure you're using the right pillow at night. Back sleepers need different pillows from side sleepers and those with chronic pain may need body pillows, cervical spine pillows or other sleeping aides that fall outside of the normal standard pillow in a department store. All these things should be common sense, but you might be surprised how many people make do with what they have long after the days of comfort and support are gone. Get into the mindset of self-care on all levels and you will always attract what you need.

Layout

Another crucial aspect of your bedroom design concept, the layout of furniture can make an amazing difference to the way you feel in your personal space. On an energetic level, whenever we move things around, we change the flow of what's incoming and outgoing. Most people won't deny the immediate realization in a room when something has shifted. For myself, if you move a rock or neglect to replace that magazine, I am going to know about it. Call it intuition or an overzealous awareness, but it's a natural way us humans keep tabs on what's around us and helps us discern when something is amiss. We are more intuitively aware of these subtleties that we realize, and there is something hardwired into our instinctual natures that keeps us on high alert for changes to our immediate environments.

These same instincts govern our comfort levels when it comes to bed placement, and most people need to see the door and window from the bed location. This is likely a precautionary sense to be on the lookout for possible danger—something highly primitive that we all still possess. Many people also prefer the bed placement on the same wall as the entry door, possibly to keep themselves less visible from the hall, or hidden from sight in the event of an intruder.

Whatever the motivator, we all create, on some level, a space that meets a psychological need, or one that reflects an emotional barrier. There are of course several feng shui rules regarding bed position and other related furniture, but many interior designers find a good design evolves effortlessly when tackled with a more organic approach to furniture placement, and I completely agree.

Every home and bedroom are different and will have its own set of possibilities, challenges, and quirks. Your job as a spiritual designer is to home in on what layout will bring you the most peace and what elements work for your specific well-being requirements amid your specific architectural dynamics and budget.

When planning your bedroom, pay attention to these tips for better energy flow and a heightened sense of security and comfort.

Make the bed the center of attention. It is, after all, the most important furniture you will ever buy so why not show it off. Place the bed in the command position so it's visible and prominent when you walk in, but if you have the luxury of great views from your bedroom, have the bed face this way for optimal serenity and amazingness.

It is generally considered best to leave a space on either side of the bed for getting in and out. If room allows, add a table with soft lighting on both sides, creating symmetry and convenience. This layout encourages companionship in the feng shui tradition, but even if you enjoy your bedroom all to yourself it still adds a great flow and pleasing visual aesthetic.

If space permits, make a place to sit. Having a separate place to read, meditate, write, or just sit with a cup of tea is always a nice addition to a bedroom. An oversized chair or chaise lounger will offer a private escape to rest your mind and body before going to sleep. As an alternative, you might consider a meditation corner to use up some extra space. Either way, the goal here is to make room for peaceful activities

If you're a feng shui follower, you'll want to keep the bed away from a bathroom wall. Going to sleep close to the loo, and all that flushing water, can have a negative impact on your energy levels. If you do not have options in this case, do some research for feng shui "cures" that might alleviate this problem.

Keep the flow open and ensure you are not tripping over things to get to your bed. From an instinctive perspective, you should be able to get up and get out in the event of an emergency. Keep the furnishings light and positioned in such a way as to compliment the space, not inhibit it. If that comfy sofa is blocking a path, try an armchair instead. Remember the goal of good design, and spiritual design, are about the flow of positive energy above all else.

You probably won't have a ton of guests in your bedroom (and if you do, that is entirely your business), but the bedroom is your personal sanctuary, and you deserve it. Consider it your temple and allow your inner voice to lead you in the most blissful design directions.

Children's Bedrooms

A child's bedroom is more than a place to sleep. It is where kids learn the *value* of sleep, the importance of rest, and the magical mystery of the dream worlds. The biggest mistake I see in people's homes, however, is the over-cluttering of a kid's bedroom. The bedroom often spills over into toy storage, art center, and stuffed animal warehouse. Understandably, many families do not have the luxury of offering three different rooms to their kids, myself included, but there are simple ways you can utilize their bedroom space, and other small spaces around the home, to keep the room for sleep as relaxing as can be.

Bedtime battles are among the most challenging aspect of parenthood and this section in no way pretends to open that can of worms on any real scale. As a parent, I believe that giving kids a wonderful, peaceful place to begin their relationship with sleep is a really good way to start. Obviously, there are other factors—like overall health, nutrition, parental influence, external circumstances etc.—that can disrupt a good sleeping experience. This section though, emphasizes the physical environment of a child's bedroom and what impact it can have on overall enjoyment and well-being and does not include other life factors for simplicity's sake (and the fact that I am not a medical specialist.)

Just like us grown-ups, kids also need a place to unwind. There should be a quiet space for them to feel rested at the end of each day, even if they're sharing a room with a sibling. If you must bunk more than one child in the same room, make some clear divisions so there is some much-needed private time for everyone. Using room dividers is a great way to separate space, as is the use of curtains or tapestries. Siblings are often desperate for some individual room, so make sure your decorating plans include something for everybody.

Before you start adding things to your cart, however, make sure you gather some wish lists when beginning your redecorating journey and allow your kids to look at rooms in magazines with you. You'd be surprised at what your little ones might gravitate toward, and you will gain some new insight into what energies they might be craving in their lives.

My own daughter shares my love of faux fur blankets, pillows, and rugs. When given some free rein to redesign her room, her tastes were far more sophisticated than I would have expected for a five-year-old. Give your own kids some design credit and let their personal expression flourish. You might have a grand four-poster bed picked out with sheer drapes and tasseled pillows to match, but your little princess may be more excited for a rustic look, with bears on her bedding and fur at her feet. Let them lead but know where to draw the line and make a room that is fun, personal, and practical.

The same care should also be given to your child's mattress and bedding selections, and keeping them in good shape will nurture their slumbering journeys. Let them try different pillows and gauge their sleeping habits to optimize comfort. If they heat up during the night, keep the window cracked or a fan set on low. If they sleep light, use a noise machine or fan to drown outside disturbance. Just like you, every little person finds their own perfect solitude so you may have to go along a few different paths with them until they find theirs. Remember—you have had many years to figure out what *you* need, but your kids are just getting started.

Feng Shui for the Bedroom

This is another one of those rooms you want to take extra special care for when spiritually optimizing your home. In feng shui, and every other design philosophy, the bedroom is supposed to be a restorative place, not the second living room or the home office or the private gym. Of course, there are many people that double up the bedroom due to a lack of space around the house, or due to a need for privacy, but the focus of your bedroom should be to rest, decompress and sleep.

The placement of the bed is the most important here, and it is generally recommended that you keep your bed as close to a stable wall as possible. With the head supported from behind, there is a feeling of security that allows a more peaceful sleep. This placement also ensures that chi in the room does not move around you too much while you're sleeping.

You should try to place your bed in the "command" position, which allows you to see the door from bed while not directly facing it. A bed facing the door in the "coffin" position is considered bad feng shui and should be avoided completely. This position is associated with death, not a good way to retire in the evening.

The best type of bed in feng shui is a solid wood or upholstered headboard. Bed frames with open slats are said to let energy dissipate and even replicate the look of a cage or jail cell. If you're going headboard free, you can create one using some clever ideas you find while doing your visual research, such as wood slats on the wall, an old mantle, or even a nice piece of artwork. Remember not to hang heavy objects over the bed, as this can leave you feeling uneasy while you sleep, especially if you live in a high earthquake zone like me.

Neutral colors are usually the best choices for a bedroom palette as discussed earlier in our color exploration section. Keep the tones soft and relaxing, like the color of sand, your morning latte, or a creamy white. This is especially true for children's bedrooms, and colors should be kept quiet and restful for little brains trying to unwind after a busy day. The less stimulation your mind has at night, the better.

Which brings us to the home office and private gym.

If you're one of those folks that likes to hibernate in your room to work on their manuscripts to avoid hearing the tv in the other room, I get it! But make sure the desk is away from the bed and not the last thing you see while going to sleep. Seeing the desk reminds us of how much work we must do the next day and will nevertheless keep up from resting soundly. It also tends to turn a very private space into a public one. If you absolutely must keep a desk set up in the bedroom, try adding one of those great room dividers to keep the office area in its own setting to separate your sleeping world from your impending deadlines.

Some final bedroom tips from the feng shui experts include keeping mirrors out of the space due to the high yang energy, keeping all electronics out of the bedroom because of all those frequencies being emitted, and keeping things in pairs to encourage partnerships. Having enough space on either side of the bed is also a must if you're in a relationship or are hoping to establish one. If only *you* can get in and out of bed comfortably, think of the symbolism behind that in the broader sense of your personal life.

Final Bedroom Tips

Make the bed. Consider it good practice to make your bed every morning when you get up. Not only is it a good psychological boost to move forward with your schedule, it's also super nice to see a cozy warm bed ready for you at the end of a long day. This is a great way to get the kids moving in the morning too and will give them a sense of accomplishment before breakfast.

Keep it tidy. Another no brainer but keep laundry off the floor or strewn across the bed. If you're one of those people that rushes outfit choices last minute, keep a hamper close by to store clothes until you have time, or desire, to put them away.

Add storage. Install some good organization units in the closets to keep clutter at bay. A room filled with mess will hamper a restful night's sleep. If your closet is perpetually messy, at least keep the door closed. Out of sight and out of mind is still better than a face full of tomorrow's to-do list.

Keep the electronics out. Gadgets emit blue light that can disrupt the release of melatonin. Using electronics before bed can prevent you from falling asleep, so it's best to keep them off at bedtime, especially for children. I am an advocate for keeping TVs and computers out of kid's bedrooms altogether. Not only does it allow them to find alternate ways to rest before sleep, but it allows greater supervision as to what they might be getting up to. Buzzing electronics are not your friend when your brain is trying to rest. Watching TV or looking at a screen before bed can negatively impact your ability to both asleep and maintain a healthy sleep cycle. Any electronics that must be in the bedroom at night should at least be turned off or kept away from your bed.

Crystals for the Bedroom

The best crystals to keep at the bedside include amethyst for its calming effects, rose quartz for its peaceful and loving energy, and selenite for its ability to bring about peace. Selenite lamps are hugely popular and add a beautiful soft glow to any room.

Deities for the Bedroom

Another Greco-Roman favorite was the goddess Hera, or Juno in later Roman religion. She was queen of the gods, and worshipped as a protector of women, childbirth, marriage, the home, and the family, making her a powerful deity for protecting the home. Hera was regarded as a being to keep on your good hearth side for she ensured the happy, healthy relationships that keep a family thriving. Her traditional symbols include the pomegranate, lily, and the peacock.

From the Nordic tales of old, the goddess Frigg was the mother of all gods, Queen of the Aesir and wife of Odin. She was a goddess of the sky, but her primary mythologies focus on her role as goddess of marriage, domestic arts and household management making her a popular choice for a guardian of the household. Frigg is often called upon to aid in childbirth, strengthen familial bonds during times of conflict, and to help maintain an orderly, peaceful home front. She is a protectress of children and women and has a strong connection to spinning and weaving. Some of Frigg's symbols include the birch tree, the Norse spinning wheel, and the hearth.

EXERCISE
Ending the Day

This exercise will help you transition your body, mind, and spirit from day-to-day activities to the world of restorative sleep. I believe that one of the biggest reasons for improper sleep is the inability for people to let go and unwind (assuming medical conditions have been ruled out).

Start this exercise by putting on comfortable clothes. Make sure the kids are in bed, your teeth are brushed, and you're ready to end the day knowing you are satisfied you will not have to get back up to turn something off or put food away or take the dog out to pee one more time.

Now, you're going to sit or lay comfortably in bed or on a chair. Do some deep breathing here to decompress and with each breath think about some aspect of the day that you are ready to leave behind. Tasks, shopping, clients, chores—breathe them all out. They are no longer a part of your day and will not be invited into your sleep time. Find a mantra here that will strengthen this idea and begin to shift focus onto what you would like to get out of your sleep.

This may seem like a silly thing to say, but most people do not go to bed with thoughts about the quality of their slumber, but rather about how the next day is going to play out. Make it a bedtime routine to actively and consciously embrace rest, embrace dreams, and allow your body and mind to restore themselves.

Once you have your thoughts calm and ready to focus on the night ahead, get your space ready for sleep. Prepare the bed, fluff the pillows, set the room's temperature, and make sure all electronics are removed from the room if possible. At the very least, they should be turned off and hidden from view. When you finally do hop into bed, allow yourself to feel the absolute comfort and joy of rest and remind yourself how amazing it is to let the body relax.

If you make it a ritual to consciously prepare for sleep, you will benefit more from the peaceful haven you have created for yourself. Your bedroom, after all, is designed for a good night's sleep so ensure you are using it to its full potential.

The Baths

Cleansing from the Outside In

....

Bathing is one of those things we cannot live without, and one of life's most celebrated pleasures. Have you ever watched a bird splash in a pool of water, or a cat spend seemingly half of its life grooming itself? Cleansing is as much a part of our spiritual nature as it is our biological drive and has always been an integral part of human civilization. The ancient Greeks and Romans were devoted bathers, and today, people in India still make ritual of bathing in the River Ganges.

So how do you, amid the chaos of daily modern living, capture the simplicity and sacredness of bathing? How do you turn your washing room into a spa-like retreat? How can you really experience the psychological and spiritual bliss of a bathtub in today's hectic world? Do not think of your bathroom as just a place for the toilet. Consider it a gateway to a world of relaxation, purification, and inner peace, just as the ancients once did. When you connect with water on a spiritual level the entire experience of the bathroom changes entirely.

131

When designing a new bathroom, renovating the one you have, think first of how you plan to use it. Many countries keep the toilet separate from the bath and shower—a design choice I feel makes much more sense. From a functional point of view placing the toilet in its own room allows people to use it even if someone is showering or using the tub. If you have this luxury when space planning, it's certainly worth exploring, leaving you a beautiful blank canvas to create a bathing sanctuary of your own.

In the West, toilets in the bathroom are the norm, so do not feel discouraged if you must work with this layout. If you feel like hiding the toilet, or if reducing its appearance is right for you, a pony wall could be the answer. I have also successfully redesigned bathroom cabinetry to reduce the "toilet in your face" problem when walking in the door. Some people are not bothered by it, but for others it detracts from the sensation of immersing yourself in cleanliness and serenity.

If you are working with a builder or contractor, discuss options for fixture placement. In many cases adding a wall or partition is a simple fix, giving you the privacy for a separate bathing experience.

It's also a good idea to consider your preferred bathing methods while you're ripping everything apart. Some people are hard-core bath enthusiasts, which might require a luxurious clawfoot or other freestanding tub to take center stage. I know many others, though, who would sacrifice a tub altogether for an amazing shower adventure. If the space permits for both, you have so many great options for a rejuvenating spa retreat, and if you consider how much time you spend here, it's well worth the money.

Atmosphere

Most people, however, never find the time or budget for a complete bathroom overhaul, but that does not mean you cannot have a great place to enjoy some TLC. There are many ways to set the tranquil atmosphere of a spa-like retreat and encourage positive chi to flow through your bathroom. Here are some tips for creating a soulful restorative space, no matter what your budget might look like.

Make It Classy

If you surround yourself with the luxury of good towels, essential oils, and other items of pampering, you will send out the message to the universe that you *know* you are worth exceptional things. Surround yourself with the best of self-care and take to the showers with the intention of restoration. Remember, intention sits at the core of how your home works for you. Make it the best you can, and it will provide you with endless avenues for joy, peace, and comfort.

Bring in the Trees

Or at least the small plants. Plants are widely loved for their air-purifying qualities alongside their obvious beauty. Some plant species thrive in high humidity areas and make great additions here. Begonias, bamboo, ferns, and Chinese evergreen are a few plants that thrive in the warm, humid, and low light conditions of most bathrooms.

Add Some Luxury

Just like the baths of the wealthy in ancient times, make your bathroom a place to indulge the senses. Light some candles, fire up the jacuzzi and let yourself languish in the warmth of a sea of bubbles. If you make yourself aware of the soothing properties of water while bathing, you will enhance the benefits of the experience.

Next, try incorporating natural elements such as wood and stone where you can. Nature brings an effortless sense of peace to any room and will boost that rejuvenating feeling.

Feng Shui for the Bathroom

In the ancient and fascinating tradition of feng shui, the bathroom is one of those iffy spots that often requires a ton of work and cures. Because water represents wealth, abundance, and career success, and the bathroom being a room filled with receptacles draining water away, this seems to be a problem. All that water going down drains symbolically means you are unwittingly losing positive chi, and subsequently all that cash flow. Obviously, that is not what you want, so paying close attention to this area is a good design idea.

It should be noted, though, that the ancient Chinese bathroom was probably nothing like the spa-like retreats being imagined in the modern world, so what was once likely a room not to linger around has become a restful place to wash, relax, and cleanse the day away. Making your bathrooms something to enjoy is a great start to balancing out the water loss effect and create a space that welcomes good vibes from the get-go.

If you are building a new home, and are inclined to follow the rules of feng shui, you will no doubt have your bathroom locations mapped out accordingly and your optimal directional placements well researched. Many of us, however, must work with what we've got, and there are many ideas to remedy the "money going down the toilet" thing.

A few of the better-known cures are:

Keep the toilet seats closed. This will stop the energy of wealth from seeping away on you.

Keep the doors closed. When not using your bathroom, keep the doors closed to stop unnatural chi from circulating around the home.

Hide the toilet. Making the toilet invisible from the doorway is a good feng shui move. Consider a dividing wall in the bathroom to keep it separated from the bath or shower if you're in the position for some renovation work.

Keep it clean! Like your other rooms, but only a bit more crucial for optimal health and positive energy. Keep your bathrooms clean and free of clutter to help create and nurture that replenishing and restorative feeling you're going for. It's also beneficial to toss any old cosmetics or hygiene products that are old or expired. Old towels can be repurposed as cleaning rags and new, fresh towels brought in. Keeping worn out and unused items in the bathroom further adds the overall energy of deteriorating well-being.

Crystals for the Bathroom

Selenite is considered a good choice for the bathroom due to its cleansing abilities. Selenite candle holders make excellent choices for bathroom decor and clean, pure energy but remember to keep it away from water as it dissolves when wet.

EXERCISE
Going with the Flow

Aside from all the implications of the bathroom in feng shui, it is still an important space in any home. This exercise is more of a daily practice, and I encourage this as a regular self-awareness, or check in, to make sure you're staying focused on your well-being.

You can do this each time you have a shower, or a bath, or any time you engage in some form of self-care regimen. It may seem silly on the surface, but many people fail to really tune into their bodies regularly which often leads to exhaustion, illness, or other symptoms of poor self-care. This could be due, in large part, to our standard of living—one that pushes us to push ourselves to the point where little daily rituals of pampering are just too exhausting.

Before you bathe, start by noticing how you feel before you begin. How does your hair feel? Is it dry and frizzy? Oily and heavy? What about your skin? Is it smooth? Tanned only on the feet? Are your nails clean? Legs hairy? Many of these things might be true, and if you garden the way I do, there will always be dirt under your fingernails.

But now you're going to move into the mindset of a refresh. The water is warm and flows effortlessly before you. It is a gift given to you in this very moment and every drop is symbolic of supply, resource, and comfort.

Notice how your skin responds the moment it touches the water. Does it feel cool? Or does the temperature seem to melt your muscles into a blissful submission? Stay with these sensations momentarily. Then, start letting the normal mind chatter back in, or the daily to-do list, or the list of phone calls you must make as soon as you get into the office, or all the stuff you never had time to finish before bed. Imagine all those things are sticking themselves to your physical body. They are like specks of dirt resting on the surface of your skin, and they are annoying.

Now, let the water take on the task of slowly washing these away, one by one, and down into the drain. Let each drop wash over you and feel how much lighter you become as the water trickles down.

Do this in the morning to clear your mind for the day ahead, or at night to free your busy brain for a restful night's sleep. This works in the shower or bath—the key idea here is how you envision the water and its effect upon your patterns of thought.

When you're done, notice the changes you feel both physically and psychologically. Has your energy level shifted? Your focus renewed?

Being mindful of the way water alters our moods and thoughts is an invaluable tool for daily meditation practices. Try this, or a similar exercise, for a week to transform your relationship with water forever.

CHAPTER TEN

The Living Room

Getting Cozy with the Elements

....

Historically known under a plethora of different names, such as the parlor room, sitting room, reception room and drawing room, the modern "living room" has undergone dramatic transformations throughout its exciting design history. What are now epicenters of familial relaxation and entertainment originated from spaces only designated to greet company or entertain guests.

Many cultures had rooms dedicated to these purposes, in fact, but in many cases, it was only those of upper-class society who could relish in this abundant luxury. Being elite meant having many people to impress, so there had to be several places to show off the latest in rare furnishings, sculpture, art and finely crafted furniture pieces.

Many of my older clients still maintain rooms such as these, not so much out of practicality but more for a sense of formal nostalgia. If you can make a room like this without some of the more modern technological distractions, it could be a wonderful place to read, write, or even have a chat with an old friend.

The real modern-day living rooms as we know them today evolved rapidly from around the 1930s onward. Before television, families gathered around the radio every evening to listen to the day's news and sports outcomes. Sofas were not widely used in these early days of modern living, and more commonly chairs were placed appropriately close to allow for ease of listening. When the dawn of television invaded the home, furniture remained centered upon this easy access for viewing. Without remote controls, someone had to be ready to always adjust the dials.

The greatest evolution of the living room, and the world of interiors, spanned from about 1945 to 1970, where artistic movements molded interior design in America. Mid-century was born. Furniture became art, and the ever-changing dynamics of this multifunctional room became embedded into the world of interiors in a way both unique and completely open to personal interpretation.

Most people are quite fond of their living rooms and spend many hours of the day here. It is one of the most fun rooms to design and decorate and usually showcases the home's overall vibe more than any other space. With the trending "cloud sofas" on the rise and our cultural obsession with visual entertainment, there seems little reason to leave the living room at all sometimes.

So, how do you make this optimal family gathering place so optimally cozy in the first place? Is there a secret way of arranging furniture, selecting accessories, and placing objects that makes this such a welcoming place to retire and snuggle up?

You bet there is!

Setup

The very first thing you should feel when you walk into a living room is a sense of wanting to be there. I know it sounds crazy, but rooms can repel a person as much as a foul odor. Crafting a place that *invites* is just as much about intuition as it is skill.

Good design is about creating feelings of comfort, order and harmony, and most interior designers and decorators come to the industry imbued with an innate sense of intuitive space planning already. It's like an unspoken superpower, but one that can also be learned with the right instruction and exercises.

Sometimes you just know which pieces will work together and where best they will dazzle your friends. Other times you're going to fumble, and that is how most designers really learn. Did I ever tell you about my experiment in re-creating ancient Rome in *my* living room when I was twenty?

There's a good reason I did not.

But back to *your* living room…

First, do some planning. Only you know what your family likes to do in their spare time. Only you know how the kids are likely to play, sit, make a mess and tumble around. Make a list of how the space is most likely to be used and make that your strategic angle.

Analyzing the dynamics of the room is a great place to start, so creating a layout that allows for the effortless flow of traffic is essential for a space that feels inviting, relaxing, and purposeful. Optimize windows for light and seating. Be mindful of common entry points and resist the urge to block off important pass-throughs with furniture. This is where you can be creative and change, direct and manipulate the flow of traffic, but at the same time nobody should be tripping over chairs or ottomans to make their way to their favorite window seat.

You can try some helpful feng shui tips and tricks here for optimizing the room's chi, or just play around with different ways of arranging furniture until the space starts to make sense. I personally try several layouts until it all just falls together, relying on the general feeling and energy patterns with each attempt at perfection. A room that works well will always have an aura of calm about it, even if you had to ask for help moving the sectional eight different times.

A room that functions at optimal levels has a few key elements: good scale, good placement, and good selections. Chunky armchairs are always warm and inviting choices, alongside those hard to resist oversized sectionals. But if your space is small, crowding in large furniture will dwarf the room. Always fit the furniture to the space, not the other way around. You should be able to walk around chairs and tables freely without hitting knees or stubbing toes. If you have the space for larger furniture, break up the room with different pieces, always leaving plenty of walking room.

Trial and error can be helpful here. I once discovered the inappropriateness of a misplaced ottoman skipping to the window to see an owl outside. By the time I completed the obstacle course, it had vanished and the ottoman in question relocated to the other side of the room.

A well-planned room will also have a great selection of multi-purpose pieces. Mix up the sectionals with a pair of armchairs, poufs that double as extra seating, and tables that could also be pieces of art when not holding drinks or magazines. Logs are a great choice for end tables and always a favorite for rustic and country decor.

Vibe

This is going to be one of those rooms where vibe, or atmosphere, are extra important. You may entertain many different pastimes here, with family, friends, or by yourself so make sure you add not just comfort, but interest as well.

Country and boho style are among favorites for living room design because of their relaxed and laid-back energies. As discussed in their individual sections earlier, choose a selection of unique pieces to create an inviting casual charm, and indulge in cozy textures for added spiritual and psychological nourishment.

It's no surprise these design trends are among the highest replicated, given their focus on embracing the simple, joyful life surrounded by natures finest. With the modern world showing no signs of slowing down, these interior dialogues between you and natural, raw materials will keep you grounded when the rush of daily life takes its toll.

Your vibe may also fall under several other interior design energies, but the main thing to remember is to keep the patterns you're creating neutral. Avoid overstimulating your family and guests with excessive electronics, too many knickknacks, or overly aggressive colors. It's all right to show off your favorite art, or that prized collection of dragon figurines—but do so tastefully, moderately, and within the overall framework of the vibe you're going for.

Seating

If you've got chronic loungers or Olympic grade sofa bouncers, make the living room as family friendly as you can. Your careful selections should include someplace comfortable, like a sectional or plush sofa that more than one person can lounge around on. Sectionals are also great for kids to jump on, practice their gymnastics, and if it's soft enough, you might just entice an unexpected afternoon nap. Thankfully, there is no shortage of apartment-sized sectionals for those with smaller living room space, or for anyone splitting the living room into separate functional spaces—like a home office.

There should also be seating geared up for activities like reading, playing a game of chess, or watching television. Accent chairs come in all shapes and sizes, as do recliners, poufs, ottomans, and chaise loungers. Giving your family room definition by offering multiple seating areas is a great way to invite leisure, relaxation, and an overall energy of rest and play.

Try offering a mix of different chairs, too, and avoid an overplanned and overcalculated look, even if you're designing within the parameters of the traditional style. Your keyword here is *relaxed*. You want to make your family and friends *really* want to hang out so avoid the "waiting room" look and try choosing chairs that are unique, stylish, and comfortable. Remember, this room is primarily for you and your family to enjoy so skip the formalities and break out the throw blankets.

If you have a fireplace, have seating nearby for those quiet celebrations of hygge discussed earlier. Place armchairs on either side for those cold winter nights and have pillows and blankets within reach for extra warmth and comfort. In the warmer months, candles can replace the heat of the fireplace, inviting more of those great moments to enjoy a late evening conversation during the shorter nights of summer.

I have learned a great deal from watching my family, and although my obsession for throw pillows has no boundaries, children seem to derive endless amusement from seeing them all over the floor. It's another one of life's great mysteries, but pillows are there to be enjoyed by everyone, on the furniture or on the floor.

Poufs and ottomans are among the most versatile little additions to your living room. For resting feet, occasional seating, afternoon tea or an unexpected game of "The Floor Is Lava," a pouf can be a family's best friend. Having a few different sizes is handy too, and whenever I see one at my local home décor store for a good price and in the right color, I bring it home.

Lighting

As discussed previously, lighting is a crucial aspect of a peaceful and nourishing design. Once you have your seating placement pinned down, make sure your lighting choices support the areas you've created for things like reading, television, or napping. Try different arrangements and combinations of overhead lighting, floor lamps and table lamps to create a balanced effect. Never leave a corner dark and ensure artificial lighting does not take precedence over natural sunlight during the daytime hours.

The Hearth

Probably the most beloved and celebrated aspect of the traditional living room is a roaring fireplace, conjuring up our deepest sense of comfort and safety.

To the ancients, the hearth was the spirit of the family and its home. It created focus and a lingering generational connection between the family and its patron gods and goddesses. Being the main source of heat for most homes throughout the ancient world, the hearth was where offerings and prayers were made to ensure the continued protection and health of one's kin.

The Greek goddess Hestia and her Roman counterpart Vesta were worshipped for centuries as one who looked over the household and all its domestic activities. In ancient Rome, the hearth fire was not only essential for cooking food and heating water, but also served as the gathering place for the family and, in time, became associated with the spirit of that family gathered around that particular hearth.[23]

....

23. Joshua J. Mark, "Vesta," World History Encyclopedia, last updated September 2, 2009, https://www.worldhistory.org/Vesta/.

In many homes today, the fireplace (wood burning or gas) takes a central focus in design, calling back to a very primal link between the hearth fire and our ability to thrive. I never advocate for the television as the main focal point of a room, and any design that wraps around the fireplace instead offers a greater, more spiritually optimized home.

If you have a fireplace, draw the eye toward it with a meaningful piece of art and some comfortable chairs close by. Sitting beside a fireplace is such a peaceful, effortless comfort that has deep psychological benefits. If your home is devoid of a hearth, substitute with an electric one to create the ambience of an open, crackling flame. Today's modern selection of wall mounted gas fireplaces work just as well and offer more convenient ways to enjoy the simplicity of a fireplace without the work (and safety concerns) of open wood burning designs.

Unlike many of the other rooms in your home, the living room will normally see heavier traffic and more diverse flows of energy. In some smaller homes, as well as apartments or condos, it is the first room you see when you walk in. Creating the right atmosphere will go miles in influencing how you and your company perceive the rest of your home, so try and put some thoughtful effort into just how this room will unfold and how best it can serve you and your family.

Feng Shui for the Living Room

The feng shui you apply to your living room is effortlessly practical from a design perspective. While feng shui have some general rules for boosting your family's relaxation room, most of the principles can be applied with your newfound intuitive decorating abilities. But before you go crazy renovating this room, or any room, make sure you know what area of the bagua map it falls on so that you can play up the best elemental energies from the get to. This is a great starting point for color scheme and the types of materials you will want to incorporate.

When you know what element you're in, make sure you choose wall colors that are supportive of the areas of your life you are hoping to activate. Refer to the color meditation exercise in chapter three to get in touch with your personal responses to each shade. If your living room rests within the fame area but you respond poorly to red, then go for hues less vibrant but still carrying the dynamic energy of fire. You can always leave walls neutral and add your zest through furniture, accessories, and art.

Furniture placement is also a large consideration for good living room feng shui and must accommodate a more public appearance than some other rooms of the home. Make sure you arrange furniture to coax out some good conversation and avoid having all the seating facing the TV. When furniture shopping, pick pieces that can accommodate everyone, too, from the jumpy toddler to the parent with the bad back, your living room should be a place of respite and make everyone feel welcome.

And a few more good feng shui tips:

Keep the flow going. Arrange furniture so that nothing interferes with the flow of chi passing through. I often use a mental exercise of imagining a gust of wind floating through my rooms. If I were chi, what would I bump into? If you must stop, make a sharp turn and go another route that is going to dissipate energy and momentum very quickly.

Artwork is a wonderful way to add some interest to your living room but should be chosen with intent and purpose. Depending on what element your living room is ruled by you can choose art that incorporates the specific colors and energies to maximize its overall effect. Go for images that invoke special feelings for you and your family instead of something just to fill up wall space.

Finally, keep the room as clutter free as possible. There may be a steady rotation of people in this room, but it's always a good idea (and even better feng shui) to clear out the space regularly. Keep windows and curtains open as much as possible too and allow the fresh chi to invigorate the space at least once a day.

Crystals for the Living Room

Amethyst, again, is a great choice for these high traffic rooms, encouraging calmness and the pursuit of higher ideals. Clear quartz too is a great energy amplifier, so can bring this room an aura of clarity for conversations with its amethyst counterpart. Add some black tourmaline as well to keep quarrels from brewing between family members in such close quarters.

Deities for the Living Room

In the mighty realm of Greek mythos, the goddess Hestia was the premier deity of the hearth and home and in the later Roman transition, she was known as Vesta, the guardian of the Roman people. The household fire was such an integral and important aspect of daily life in the ancient world that they worshipped and honored these deities as guardians over its ongoing flame. To keep the home fire burning and hot was religious duty, political duty, and something that ensured the continuity of both domestic and state affairs. The sacrificial fires were crucial to keeping the deities happy and appeased and were a foundation for the strength of the city-state.

Honoring the goddess Hestia or Vesta meant an obligation to host and shelter visitors and turning away a stranger in need was sure to invoke the wrath of this goddess. Her traditional symbols as Hestia are fire, cows, and pigs, which also represented domestic wealth throughout much of the ancient world, while Vesta was usually associated with the donkey.

Inviting the goddess Hestia or Vesta into your home will ensure a loving sense of sanctuary and safety and instill the peace and comfort of being home. A bust of the goddess on the mantel or at the front door is a great way to honor this deity's energy, and a clean working fireplace, or a collection of candles, will bring your home the warmth that she promises.

The most potent and worshipped of the pagan deities, Brigid was the Irish goddess of inspired craft and wisdom, stirring the fires of creativity to those who called upon her. Known as a triple goddess possessing the fire of the hearth, the fire of the forge and the fire of inspiration, Brigid was a fierce protector of the home and for all who sought the creative spark to bring forth invention and creation. Her name means "exalted one" and she survived and thrived as one of the most celebrated deities throughout the Celtic pagan world, still celebrated today on Imbolc. As a powerful immortal being she is the embodiment of the element of fire and this Lady of the Flame brings warmth and light to the home.

Symbols for Brigid include fire, serpents, and Brigid's cross, which was hung on front doors during pagan times to protect the home from fire. Here is an incantation to call upon the great goddess of fire to bless your new abode:

May Brigid bless the house wherein you dwell
Bless every fireside, every wall and door
Bless every heart that beats beneath its roof
Bless every hand that toils to bring it joy
Bless every foot that walks its portals through
May Brigid bless the house that shelters you.[24]

....
24. Ireland Calling, "Brigid's Cross (Brighid's Cross, St. Brigit's Cross)," accessed February 2021, https://ireland-calling.com/brigids-cross.

EXERCISE
Experiments with Space

I have spent more time with this exercise over the course of my life than most, but it is a great way to teach yourself about not just furniture placement, but of the importance of good flow in a larger room. If you're starting a living room design from scratch or just doing some shuffling around, this exercise will be a great opportunity for you to really learn your room and what you can gain the most from best placement.

I always start the exercise the same way, by standing at the doorway of the living room and just looking. Sometimes I do this for a very long time, allowing a few different layouts to pop into my head to try. Oftentimes, I spend more time on this part than moving things around, but you will find your own way of tuning into your space as soon as you begin.

The key focus for doing this is to start visualizing how the room works. Where are windows in relation to doors, staircases, other rooms in the house? Where does the best light come in? Where do people generally gravitate when they are in the room?

Once you have watched the room for a few minutes, or over the course of a few days, you should have a couple of ideas ready to implement. The biggest thing to set first should be your seating, so play around with sofa and chair placement before setting down the smaller details. Whether you have a large sectional or a collection of cozy armchairs, sit in each one when placed and see what you notice about each. Many people neglect this part, and often the chairs we never sit in ourselves are not in optimal arrangement. Have a seat on each part of the sofa as well to get a feel for what your family members, or guests, are likely to experience from that one spot. If you have ever watched *The Big Bang Theory*, you will get this. I always find it interesting how different every spot in a living room feels. Lighting, air flow, heat from a fireplace, what's in the immediate visual field. It's worth the exploration and could mean a lot more comfort for your company.

When you get this pinned down, lighting will be your next big challenge. Use a combination of floor lighting, table lighting and overhead lighting to achieve a balanced look. Again, you really want to watch the room from the point of entry to see where light is pooling and where you might need to turn it up.

This is where you can start adding your cozy accessories and smaller furniture pieces. Try a few different placements and walk around the room with each one. Does it make sense? Does it make the room work better? A giant coffee table in the middle of the room that no one can reach might not be the best option. Keep tables clustered next to seating areas for drinks, books, phones, remote controls or reading glasses.

The biggest point to remember during this exercise is that there should be no obstacles getting from one point to another

Fill in the blanks once your functional items have been added. Artwork, plants and flowers, books and magazines, pillows, blankets, and a few well-placed objects will add warmth and interest to your new and improved space.

CHAPTER ELEVEN

The Home Office
Become a Work at Home Guru

....

The term *home office* can mean many things to many people and working from home has taken on such an exciting role in today's bustling world. Online business continues to boom, and many careers offer a nice flexibility in work/home opportunity. The COVID-19 pandemic, of course, shed some new and interesting light on ways to adapt to changing work environments and will leave lasting affects for years to come.

But because of the obvious challenges to working at home (naps, extra snacks, TV, kids), designing a well-planned office space is crucial to keeping your focus on your work when you need to.

A dedicated space for your career at home will enhance productivity, drive motivation, and make you forget about all of the other things you *could* be doing around the house. And we all do it. Many of us, especially me, are like puppies watching squirrels outside a window. During the writing of this book, for example, each new chapter inspired me so much I quite literally redesigned every room in my house during its production.

Every. Single. One.

But do not fret, work-at-home warriors! There are ways to maximize your space for harmony, clarity, focus, and success. It just takes some careful and thoughtful planning, determination to do the work at hand, and an environment that nurtures your working goals. So, if you are currently trying to launch an Etsy business surrounded by toys and heaps of laundry, this chapter is for you, as well as anyone making a bold effort to crush those deadlines from the kitchen table.

Granted, some of you may not be blessed with a separate room from which to craft your genius, but there are still ways to make a functional and effective space anywhere in your home. Before you get going on the shopping spree at Staples, take a good look at your current home office and ask yourself the following questions:

Is It What I Need?

We give our rooms meaning in several ways, but intention is the most powerful activator of the way you interact with your space. When designing or redecorating your home office space—wherever it may be—make sure you align it with the type of work you are doing. Artists will obviously require oodles of space for supplies and work surfaces. Writers will need several recycling bins to toss the first, second, and third drafts of their work, and home businesses are probably drowning under mountains of paperwork.

Invest in the right furniture to make working from home easy and organized, like a good filing system, bookshelves, or storage totes. If fabrics and sewing is your game, get clever with new ways to sort materials and threads that make sense to you. Sorting by color has always been a favorite of mine and is visually appealing as well as simple to maintain. If you enjoy color decorating and general organizing magic, you'll love *The Home Edit*'s Clea Shearer and Joanna Teplin. They offer fantastic ideas for keeping your home streamlined and tidy—just what you'll need to work from home successfully.

If you're a designer, keep inspirational images, books and objects close by. I keep stacks of design magazines in my home office that never fail to boost my obsession with home makeovers. Sure, they often drive me to spend more on home interiors than most normal people, but it gets the creative juices flowing, and that is really what you're hoping for here.

Inspiration

In that same perspective, do not add things to your office that you do not need, like bulky printers or scanning machines you barely use, or heaps of file folders that are likely to take up valuable space in the drawers or on the desk. Office supply stores are amazing, I know, but you probably do not need ten colors of sticky notes, five kinds of push pins, and twelve highlighters. If you absolutely do, that is amazing, but keep it organized and out of sight when not in use. Which brings us lovingly to point number two

Is It Organized?

Clutter is the number one productivity killer among work at home gurus (along with Pinterest, pets and small children). As discussed in other chapters, the existence of clutter is definitely going to impact how you tackle your work each day. If you do not know where one workday ends and the next begins, it can become an insurmountable task to stick to a schedule. Clean up your desk when you decide enough is enough for one day, and mentally shut it off. There must be some kind of separation between work and home life, especially when you're combining the two. Your family will thank you.

You will thank you. And your long-term emotional health will certainly thank you.

Is It Functional?

You're probably going to spend many hours in your home office if your livelihood is attached to it. If the office is a room unto itself, you have no excuses for underperforming furniture. If budget is an issue, at least focus on your main working area and ensure you can sit or stand comfortably while you work. If you truly want to see personal success, investing in yourself first is a key part of the puzzle. Pushing yourself to work in a run down or chaotic environment won't yield the results you are looking for but will leave you feeling drained and unhappy. Your foundation is crucial. Spend some money on the solid basics first.

If you must sit, let there be an ergonomically friendly chair in your future and a well-fashioned desk to support you on your journeys. While it can be tempting to curl up in bed with your laptop, pay attention to how this might affect your posture as well as your likelihood to take those naps I warned you about.

Again, assess the availability of daily supplies, storage, technical equipment etc. and pare it down to necessities.

And please make sure it works, too. A broken printer is a broken printer, no matter how much you paid for it five years ago.

But an office is not just a room that works well—it should be a room that feels great. Zero in on what types of energies you want hanging around while you work so hard and put together a solid plan of your optimal space. Just like the other rooms in your home, the office is a great place to flex your designer muscles. Find a style that reflects your creativity, or inspires you to write, paint, stitch, design, sell or whatever it is you're doing to bring home the bacon.

Some people enjoy the classic comfort of a traditional study or library, while others embrace a more minimalist approach. Too many objects in the office can distract you from meaningful work. But, on the other hand, they can also be good tools for getting those proverbial juices flowing. Design is subjective. Design is also a great self-exploration and can lead us down alleys we never thought we would wander down. Design preferences also tend to change over the years, and you may find yourself embracing a simple Scandinavian look where once you flourished in a neoclassical universe. Pay attention to these new areas of interest, as they can hint to aspects of yourself that are trying to find a place to explore.

Finally, try and make your office a room with a decent view of the outside world to give yourself mental breaks throughout your work and your eyes a break from the computer. Having scenery to indulge in has been proven to enhance success, but if you do not have much to look at, keep some healthy plants close by to boost productive, growing energy and keep the air in your work zone clean and fresh. Opening the window will also keep your mind sharp and alert while you toil away on that keyboard. Keeping a yoga mat handy is another great way to get those stretches in, especially if you are obligated to sit for longer periods of time.

Feng Shui for the Office

The home office, or any work office, is where you work hard to create financial wealth so it's probably on your list of most important places to get right. In feng shui, your career energy is said to be mainly in the north, is ruled by the element of water, and has some good ideas for boosting chi to get things moving in the right direction.

The first thing to remember is that the design of your office space is going to impact you tremendously for the extensive hours you spend there. Choose colors that are inspiring, soothing and grounding to help you focus on the tasks at hand. Do not choose colors so bright that they distract your attention, but rather ones that blend into the room.

Next, ensure your desk faces the door so you can see everyone who enters. This is considered the command position, like the bedroom and kitchen, and is important for maintaining a sense of control over your space. Your desk should be comfortable to work from, and in good repair always. Wood makes a great desk choice for its durability and longevity—aspects every good career should strive for.

It is also considered good feng shui to have a solid wall behind you while you work. This gives you the sense of being supported in your work and on your life path. Keeping inspiring images close by is also good practice, like photos of people who have supported your career progress or maybe even quotes that get you motivated every day to achieve your best.

You can also use your compass and map out the career sector and wealth sector of your home office, and even your desk, for adding some elemental enhancements for extra good luck. Make room too for some healthy plants that keep the air clean and instill a sense of continual upward growth.

Crystals for the Office

The best crystal for the home office is usually clear quartz for keeping the mind free from unnecessary clutter while you work. Amethyst is also a good choice for its calming and stress relieving attributes during times of tight deadlines and demanding clients.

EXERCISE
Meditation for a Booming Business

Because the home office could be the epicenter of your career success, putting the right type of energy into it is going to be paramount. You do not really want to relax here, but you also do not want to be overwhelmed with incoming inspirations from the universe, a heavy workload, or the wrong clientele. Use this meditation to help focus your intentions for business and set realistic expectations to match your current capacities.

As with all meditations, find a place to sit comfortably. Make sure you are devoid of all distractions and you're in a state of mind where you can focus on some solid visuals.

Start first by picturing yourself. You are the foundation of your career. You are what fuels its momentum and drives it forward. Your business life depends upon many things, but your own willingness to sustain your vision is what guides it to success or failure.

How do you envision yourself as you relate to your job? Confident? Capable? Exhausted? Elon Musk?

Now, imagine yourself as just you, stripping away all your preconceived notions and whimsical daydreams about millionaire status and CEO ambitions.

Just you. Just for a moment. How would you define yourself outside of your work? What makes you the greatest without money, promotions, and sales contracts? What energy do you possess? Find your core and what it is that makes you so good at what you do.

Try to remember this at least once a day.

Now that you have solidified your true creative essence, start conjuring up some images of those things that define success for you. What does it look like? Big line ups? Repeat clients? More articles? Book deals? Partnerships?

Define your business needs as images rather than detailed and complicated situations. Imagine shaking hands, signing papers, ringing up sales, talking to satisfied clients.

If you can find enough images in magazines that represent these goals and ideals, make a board for your office to keep a firm hold of what your business accomplishments look like. Our ability to create comes directly from our ability to imagine. When we can successfully see the way our dreams manifest, and begin to feel them, we can make them happen.

You can do this every day if you wish or save this meditation for times you're feeling out of sync with your path or far away from your true career goals.

CHAPTER TWELVE
Rooms for Kids
Taming the Mess Monsters

....

Kids are unique little creatures, full of an energy and natural curiosity worthy of profound envy. They are endlessly chatty, busy, messy, and self centered, but they are also growing, developing beings incredibly sensitive to their environments.

While rooms for children can be the most rewarding to design and decorate, they can also be challenging. Finding a healthy, manageable balance between creative free play and artistic explosions and a calm soothing place for their busy minds to rest can be an hourly juggling contest.

This is precisely why crafting the perfect spaces for kids is so important. If you want to eliminate some of the struggles of kid-induced chaos, there are some great ways to engage your little herd into loving their space so much, they might want to take care of it.

Yes, really!

And not only that, but you can sneak in a chance to re-live your own childhood here or give your children the room you never had.

I do not know about you, but my room as a child was no magical adventure and obviously pre-dated the era of cool spaces for kids.

It's easy, though, to fall into the pitfall of going overboard and creating rooms that are overstimulating and cluttered. Let's face it: the world of design has much more to offer today than forty years ago and if I could design a children's room every day for the rest of my life, I would be ecstatic. Maybe it's the cute woodland themes or the play teepees or the beds that look like cabins in the woods, but the stuff we can bring into the world of children's decor has reached an all-time refinement and level of fun. Today more than ever, we push our kids to explore the sensory world as if the survival of the species depended on it.

Not only can you play with a myriad of styles, concepts, textures, and colors, but you can pass along a sense of freedom, joy, and effortless peace to your kids, looking for their own unique ways to express themselves.

But before you go filling up those toy boxes and slapping on the wacky paint, let's review some important and common rooms for kids, their purpose, and how to make the most of the space without crossing energetic paths.

Kids use a lot of energy, and some rooms are designed for just that. Playrooms, arts and crafts stations, backyards. These are all great spaces to create the perfect foundations for little ones to explore the world and their individual skills just waiting to burst out.

Here are some great ways to make the most of children's rooms and encourage your little ones to engage with their space in new and meaningful ways.

Storage

Remember the chapter on space clearing, and the impact of clutter on the mind and body? Well, those same rules apply for your little ones so bring those organizing muscles back out and have the storage totes ready.

Good organization is paramount when dealing with kids' stuff and will save you and your offspring a lot of time and stress in the long run. Invest in some attractive storage units, stackable totes, and anything your child can manage on his or her own. Make it easy for them to put away their own toys by having clear areas set up for specific things. This will also give them a boost of confidence and some responsibility for their own belongings.

Puzzles there. Stuffed toys here. Dress-up clothes in *that* trunk. These are the kinds of things that help children categorize what they have, find it more easily, and learn the value of a tidy space. It also means they are learning self-control, which translates to less mess for you to clean up.

Keep it simple and try keeping messy items such as art supplies out of the bedroom unless you have room for a child size table and chairs. Arts and crafts stations can easily be set up in a separate room altogether, such as the dining room, a little alcove, the kitchen island, or anywhere that forces a regular cleaning up. Kids left alone to craft in their rooms are capable of making serious chaos and you're more likely to get that crayon on walls, Barbie hair chopped off, and stickers on the dresser. Teaching children to respect what they have will make for much more responsible adults.

Theme

Once you have successfully sorted the masses of toys and learning tools into some seriously stylish methodology, look at the overall theme of your child's bedroom.

Themed bedrooms are one of a parents' guilty pleasures, but if you're going to do it, do it with some self-restraint. Many parents go overboard with loud colors and gimmicky merchandise when trying to recreate Cinderella's castle or a mission to outer space. Go back to Pinterest. Find some good ideas that do not break the bank or overdo the disco balls. Your mission is harmony, not birthday party at the bowling alley.

And the oh-so-popular bed in a bag that adorns your child's room with the Paw Patrol. I know you love them, but you really *don't* have to buy them. This is a marketing trap and a touchy subject in design, I know, and an inexpensive way to change up the theme of your kid's room.

But.

Kids are bombarded all day with media images and TV characters and probably already own a hundred *Paw Patrol* related items. If you want to go with longevity, choose a theme they will enjoy for a while and one that grows with them. Instead of character themed bedding, go with something neutral like solid colors or gentle stars or clouds and let them keep a few favorite stuffies on the bed. Even one toss pillow with Pikachu on it is better than an entire bedding set they will be over by their next birthday. Kids live in the moment, but *you* can have some control over the longer-term investments in your kid's bedroom decor and help them separate their play and media time from the time to rest and reflect.

A child's bedroom is a good place to create a grounded, calming place to rest their growing brains and tired bodies. Choose bedding and accessories that they can love longer and won't seem too childish next year. There is nothing wrong with a themed bedroom, but going to bed in the *wild, wild, west* might be difficult for a tired little mind at the end of a long day.

Allow your child to try the color meditation exercise to see what kind of response you get. For younger kids, I have an exercise that works well for color picking. Set up a table with different color groups (this could be items of the same color, or colors in a certain palette for example), and watch to see which groups they gravitate toward. I often use toy cars grouped by colors, or even groups of paints at an art table. This may not be definitive but will show you what colors excite your child and which ones do not. If your child chooses loud and bold colors, save those for the playrooms to really get him moving and opt for softer shades of those colors for the sleeping space.

This is especially important when it comes to wall color, and I always recount the tale of my own child who slept terribly for several months until I covered up the bright yellow paint his bedroom was plastered in. These things may seem trivial to some, but to a young child something as simple as a busy bedroom could cause a host of nighttime troubles.

Having said all of that, there is still plenty of opportunity to transform the bedroom into a magical, carefree place. Princess themes are popular for girl's rooms and can be enthralling to a youngster, heightening the imagination of being in a faraway land. Forest themes are also fantastic and keep a child's wonder and enthusiasm for the natural world fresh and exciting. Even as an adult I would love a forest bedroom because I am a random stick enthusiast, remember?

Incorporate a sturdy bed that can be changed up when necessary and again, try and avoid novelties that are likely to wear off in the interest department by your child's next birthday. Canopy beds are a nice addition if room permits, and bunk beds can free up valuable floor space that can be used for important play and learning activities.

When designing, or redecorating a child's bedroom, keep the idea of rest at the forefront of your amazing and whimsical planning. It is so easy to get carried away when it comes to youth decor, but too much visual stimulation is not what you're going for here. Keep electronics such as TVs out of the bedroom, or at least provide the option to hide it away at night. Keep it natural. Keep it peaceful. Keep it tidy. And keep the high-spirited energy of the fairies at bay. They will be better suited in other rooms for kids.

Art/Teaching Rooms

All right, now you can let loose and have a bit more fun!

In the art and playrooms, it's okay to dangle giant branches or hot air balloons from the ceiling. Here is where you want to unleash the raw inquisitive nature of children and coax out all of those crazy ideas you can literally see bouncing around their heads. Think of these as educational rooms, and if you're a teacher you can incorporate many of these ideas into the classroom as well.

Add some pin boards, or clothing hanger art holders to the room. Chalk walls are always one of my favorites; I have yet to see a kid resist drawing on a chalk wall.

These are obviously great spaces to bring some nature indoors. In my daughter's arts and crafts corner, I hung a giant arbutus branch over the art table that spans most of the space, and we often craft seasonal decorations to dangle playfully from the branches. This space also doubles as a discovery center—displaying rock, crystal, seashell and stick collections along with various magnifying glasses for easy hands-on learning activities. It is also used for painting, sculpting, homeschool work, and Lego. The corner itself is just an unused space off the kitchen, so you do not need an entire room to find a kiddie corner. Just get creative.

If you are blessed with some extra space, include things like plants or seed growing experiments. Hang posters of natural earth cycles, space, and anything that showcases the magic of the natural world. The more you, as a parent, encourage interest in the planet, the more in tune your child will become. Make these exploration rooms and spaces a place to ask questions, bubble volcanoes, examine fossils, or paint with fingers.

Remember the rules of organization here as well, so that little hands can easily find the supplies they are looking for. Providing your kids with their own spaces to initiate art or learning is one of the best ways you can foster a love of independent exploration. Just like their bedroom toys, let them be responsible for keeping their things tidy and you will likely notice a new enthusiasm. This is a magic all its own for any parent.

Playrooms

If you weren't having enough fun designing those other rooms for kids, now is your chance to be bold. Playrooms can be anything from a room full of toys to elaborate portals into crazy fun dimensions. Many people choose to convert a basement or garage into the "kid's zone" which is a wonderful way to give them room to let loose, make noise, and keep the clutter out of the main living areas.

These are great places to store toys, set up different play zones, and keep the ever-changing needs of childhood contained and organized under one magical ceiling. Remember to make a regular habit of cleaning out toy bins or changing out activities and equipment your kids have outgrown or lost interest in. Keeping the playroom fresh is the easiest way to keep them engaged and excited to play.

Some of the things you can add to the playroom to amp up the fun factor include trampolines, zip lines (yes, really), bouncy castles, slides, ball pits, and tents. These are the rooms you can invite the fairies to play, because this is where those energetic little people we call offspring need to learn about the world through physical play. This is also a good time to use those bright colors or bold accessories you may have shied away from in the kids' bedrooms.

Outdoors

I am fully convinced that if most children were left to their own devices for one day, they would turn wild. Which is why the outside world is so important for their optimal development and general well-being.

This is where they can search for fairies in the tree trunks, chase butterflies, follow ants, smell grass and the aroma of flowers. Outdoor play spaces can be a gateway to the most enchanting realms and even if you do not have a private backyard, search out sacred little spots in your neighborhood and make them your own. Underneath an old tree, beside a creek, forests, beaches, hills, pumpkin patches, flower gardens.

All these places contain a magic unduplicated in the home, and will heighten mood, sharpen focus, create peace, and foster curiosity. I have a backyard the size of a sandbox, but island living means that beaches, rainforests, orcas, seals and eagles are just minutes from home. Treasure the special places you find, and never stop teaching the power and immensity of the natural world.

If you are planning an outdoor space for children, try creating a balance between structural elements and free roaming natural spaces. Swing sets, slides and trampolines are great outlets for physical play, but incorporate spaces for things like sandboxes, waterplay, and a small area for gardening. If you're lucky enough to have the perfect tree for a treehouse setup, you could be the coolest parent ever.

Look for creative ways to use the outdoor space you've got and try and envision it through the eyes of your childhood self. Among the never-ending boom of our technical society, give your kids a reason to explore the wonder of a backyard the way you did all those years ago. I can remember the thrill of climbing a tree and catching snakes in the creek down the street. What kinds of things will your own kids remember?

It should go without saying, of course, but with all these amazing new spaces for kids must also come safety. Always make sure your fun zones, art centers, and bedrooms are age appropriate. Large ball pits and bunkbeds are for older kids, so think pint-sized fun for infants and toddlers and work your way into the magic step by step. The spirit of childhood should be cultivated no matter what rooms you create for kids, now more than ever.

The world is changing, and the children of today need immense support and opportunities for rest as they take on the responsibilities and dangers of a technological society. Many of us parents struggled with the onset of COVID-19 and the lockdowns and isolations that followed. However, it also granted new opportunities to fine tune our environments—similar to the way we adjusted them when our children were taking their first steps—to make our homes a reflection of what we truly want for our kids.

Keep the Lights Down

Lighting is a great way to adapt your kids to the cycles of day and night. Just like the other rooms in your home, you should adjust the lights in your child's room to ensure proper illumination for reading, and relaxing ambience for getting ready for bed. Keep curtains and blinds open during the day to take full advantage of natural light and try blackout curtains to help with a better sleep at night, especially during the summer months.

Deities for Kid's Rooms

In Slavic Paganism, the Domovoy was believed to be the spirit of a deceased member of the family. Much like the Roman belief, the departed head of the household or other kin would hang around the familial home in the form of household guardians, sometimes taking the form of an animal, sometimes as an old gray-haired man.

The Domovoy were thought to protect the well-being of the family, especially the children and animals, to ensure the longevity of the family name. The Slavs depicted their household gods as clay statuettes and each Domovoy would be shown wearing the distinct costume of the tribe to which the family belonged.[25]

EXERCISE
Sorting Fun!

This is the best exercise when undertaking a children's room makeover and really makes your kids work for their own space. Take them on a shopping trip for a good selection of bins, totes, baskets or whatever you have unanimously agreed upon for their room. Involving them in the process of organizing their own things is an important life lesson, and believe it or not, instills a sense of control of their immediate environment.

Next, have them brainstorm ideas about how to sort and categorize their things. Every mind thinks in different ways, so not all children will like their stuff laid out the same way. Some children are highly visual people, thriving on color coordination or sorting by size. Some others want their toys and supplies organized by type: puzzles together, character toys in the same tub, stuffies sorted by animal, etc. Let your children guide the sorting process to allow their unique way of processing the world develop. They may want to try more than one approach, but this is a wonderful way to teach them about how to keep focused and how to create order around them.

Encourage this often. It is a valuable life skill and should be nurtured whenever possible.

25. Jan Máchal, "Slavic Mythology" in *The Mythology of All Races. III, Celtic and Slavic Mythology*, ed. L.H. Gray (Wentworth Press: Boston,1918), 217–389.

CHAPTER THIRTEEN

The Guest Rooms
Outfitting Extra Space

Benjamin Franklin once said, "Guests, like fish, begin to smell after three days."[26]

While often true, it is a humorous far cry from the ancient Greco-Roman idea of *hospitium*, which was the notion of hospitality that played a solid role in ancient culture.

To the ancients, it was the divine duty of every host to treat his guest properly. Failing to do so would invoke the wrath of the gods and potentially break familial ties and political contracts. Hosting company, strangers or not, was embedded into cultural law and entire civilizations depended upon this code of conduct to keep peace and establish regional alliances. Food was presented, baths drawn, wine poured, and conversations could last days upon the goodwill and wealth of a noble host. Many ancients also believed

....

26. Shawn M. Burn, "The Trouble with Houseguests," Psychology Today, last updated July 25, 2013, www.psychologytoday.com/ca/blog /presence-mind/201307/the-trouble-houseguests.

that a stranger at the door needing a place to stay could be a god in disguise, and we often see this theme pop up in fairy tales throughout history. The Romans in particular had a passion for entertaining, and most villas would have offered guest rooms for those traveling from afar. They are famous for extravagant dinner parties with exotic foods and dazzling entertainment, things that many today still indulge in when gathering friends and family.

In today's world, we obviously have little in the way of political agendas or the sudden appearance of strangers landing ashore from a faraway land that may or may not be a goddess in disguise, but the idea of *hospitium* is still a part of our culture where we choose to host friends, family, or even coworkers. It signals a need to make connection, and the unspoken pledge of our company to perhaps offer the same hospitality in return one day in the future.

As hosts and hostesses in a modern world, where many relatives live across an expansive globe, inviting those we love to stay is a heartfelt experience. With this appreciation, we enter the guest rooms, poised and ready to create a calming oasis and restorative experience for company we relish in, and some we may not. Fortunately for you, interior design warrior in the making, guest rooms can be as fun as crafting children's rooms—the possibilities are endless and make great practice for honing your skills at creating intuitive spaces.

The pulling together of a guest room poses a unique challenge when following the instinctual cues talked about in this book. This is the only space not being made directly for *you*, but on many subconscious levels it is being made for *everyone*.

But guests can be so entirely different; how do you make a room for everyone? Some are die-hard homebodies, forever glued to the comforts of home. Others are adventurous and seek endless new places to spread their wings.

No matter which one of these your company tends to be, everyone at heart enjoys coming home at the end of each day to a place that feels safe, relaxing, and comfortable. As a guest in someone else's home, or in a far-off hotel somewhere in Vegas, these basic needs are always at the forefront of a getaway experience.

Even if an overnight stay is meant to be exciting and completely out of the ordinary, there are some elements that make a stay in another place memorable and inviting. When designing rooms and spaces for your own company, whether close family, or friends from out of town, here are some amazing ways to make your guests never want to leave.

Theme

Designing a guest room opens the door wide open for playing around with themes, just as we discussed with rooms made for kids. But why is choosing a theme so important? Why not just throw together a well-made bed with some well plumped pillows and call it a day at the Inn?

Because that is boring, and if you're going to share your humble or grand abode with semi-likable to lovable companions, why not show some real gusto and make it something they talk about long after their departure. The best part is, this is a room you can change up seasonally and make comfortable and fun any time of year.

Some of my favorite themes for guest rooms include the oh so cozy log cabin theme, the beach house theme, the quiet farmhouse theme, and the trendy bohemian theme. All these styles allow abundant opportunity for fresh, soft, and natural accessories that will leave company feeling well rested after their trip.

Keep in mind the energies that will play out with your design choices and avoid overstimulating themes. Ensure your color selections are toned down, to avoid some of the heavy colors that come with styles like African Safari, ancient Rome, or Oriental. While popular choices for theme rooms in hotels, in your own abode it might be more spiritually optimizing to keep it light. It will still be a room for your own family's use when company subsides so make it livable and usable on a regular basis as well.

When done right, themes can also instill in your guests the feeling of being somewhere pleasantly relaxing, like a romantic English cottage or a cabin tucked away in the woods. Depending on your decor choices, they could also bring about feelings of playfulness, adventure, or excitement. A beach-inspired room might harken visitors back to a favorite beach hang out as a kid or an exciting first vacation. An energetic, pretend trip to a log cabin might recall fond memories of early camping or ski trips—or at least muster up the feelings of being there.

Give your guests something different to indulge in while staying for the weekend and never doubt the role of atmosphere and how much it impacts the spirit. Remember, creating atmosphere is primarily an energetic undertaking influencing not just mood, but thought processes and physiological responses as well.

Incorporating those elements everyone tends to find peaceful will help your guests stay grounded while also enjoying the joys of a vacation. Add some soft, comforting accessories like sheepskin rugs, knit pillows, a favorite seashell collection, and some candles for ambience. If your guest room cannot accommodate a fireplace, an electric one will add oodles of serenity—especially on a cold evening.

For many people, theme rooms are like the fantasy play from childhood and stimulate parts of our creative brain that start to lay dormant during our more formal adulting years. Do some experimentation in your decorating undertakings. Try a few designs. Take some pictures. Have friends or family members try it on for size to see how accommodating each element feels. Keep the look informal, but do not overdo things like trinkets or unneeded accessories.

Furniture

The guest beds should be the most thoughtful additions in your guest accommodations, with some idea as to your normal company and their comfort requirements. Do you have regular visits from an older generation, like grandparents? Or do you regularly entertain other children or grandchildren on those annual family get-togethers?

Built-in bunk beds are a fantastic option if you have siblings or other close relatives arriving. Many vacation homes and family ski cabins incorporate this idea to comfortably house several people without using a large footprint. Beds tucked away into walls, with fun ladders and matching bedding make these rooms both whimsical and grounded.

Matching twin beds work incredibly well, too, and can be dressed up to accommodate whoever happens to be staying for the weekend. I make a habit of storing a few different duvet covers and toss pillows so changing up a room is a quick and enjoyable task. The benefit to keeping wall colors neutral in guest rooms means you can do a costume change whenever the desire strikes.

Gear up for a change in the fall/winter months and again for the spring/summer season. Changing decor seasonally is also a wonderful way to keep your spirit in tune with the natural cycles of the earth and will give you the chance to fully integrate the gifts and energies of each precious season into your home.

Adding a chair or two will also add some gold stars to your host rating, so be mindful of a nice cozy spot for reading, watching TV, or peeking outside at the views. Think cushy papasan chairs, beanbag chairs, swinging chairs or an oversized butterfly chair for seating that is a little different for company hoping to relax away from home.

If space is limited and you're short an extra room for the occasional drop-ins, try adding a Murphy bed or daybed to an existing home office or arts and crafts room. Rooms that can double up for company when needed mean that its yours to use every other day of the year you're not hosting and entertaining. Most people will find this a more practical solution when devoid of space. Those with apartments and condos can take full advantage of adaptable furniture, like futons and daybeds, room dividers, and curtains to create a perfect guest oasis.

Other things to add to your guest room to make a stay both comfortable and convenient might include a charging port for electronics, a full height mirror so company can prepare their travel wardrobes in private before joining you for breakfast, a private washroom, and even a portable fridge for them to keep late night drinks and snacks handy.

Crystals for Guest Rooms

Your best bets for the guest rooms are amethyst for encouraging a sense of spiritual connectedness and rose quartz for its soothing energies of love and gentleness.

Deities for the Guest Rooms

In the ancient world, the Greek god Zeus was thought to be the protector of men and gods. He was the patron of hospitality (referred to as *xenia* in Greek) as well as guests and company of all kinds. It was believed that Zeus would avenge any wrong done to a stranger, which is why the idea of being a good host took on such grave importance in society.

EXERCISE
Trying It On

I love this exercise for guest room transformations and use it often with clients as well as friends. When not being used to entertain company, the guest room can be used as sort of a practice room, whether it is an entire room strictly devoted to company, or a converted home office, library, or spare den. If you have this kind of space available to play with, it's time to have some fun!

Start by emptying the room as much as possible, except for staple furniture pieces. Go back to the first principles in this book and give it a clean, top to bottom, and set your intentions straight. If you are going to try a few different looks in this room, play around with energy forms a bit. Is this a guest room for a relative? An old friend? Children or grandparents? Use what you have learned about setting atmosphere and select your themes accordingly. It really is amazing how a room can change up its entire dynamic force just by what colors, accessories, lighting and bedding you put together.

An old friend of mine used to change up a spare room in her home roughly every three to four weeks. Nothing major, but subtle shifts in furniture, lighting placement, aromas, and differing displays of treasured collections. She invited people over shortly afterward and waited to see how the changes impacted her company. I could always spot the differences right away, of course, but most others could not, even though the room felt obviously altered from the first step in. It was a fun experiment to watch and solidified my belief that even the smallest of changes can make huge differences on levels below the surface of conscious awareness.

Try using different bedding, altering furniture placement, using different art on the walls, or different plants and flowers, enough where it feels, to you, like a totally new room.

Then, ask people to spend some time in that room, noticing with each refresh what feels comfortable, what feels forced, and which room offered the best energies for rest and relaxation.

Think of this exercise as playing dress up, but with a room instead. It's fun. Its creative. And it's this kind of expression that will help boost your ability to design and decorate intuitively. Have fun with it and offer up the room to as many people as you're willing to let hang around your house. The best part about this room is that you can deconstruct it whenever you like.

If you're in a home that does not have an extra room for company, you can still have fun creating secluded spaces for guests with the use of a room divider. Even closing off a small part of your living room for a temporary guest house can be an adventure in design. Use your creative skills, go and find some visual cues, and find amazing new ways to create a soothing space that wasn't there before.

CHAPTER FOURTEEN

Outside Spaces

Turning Wilderness into Harmony

....

Mary Cantwell once said "Gardeners, I think, dream bigger dreams than emperors."[27] And I believe it!

To jump into the all-inspiring task of taming the wild by nurturing, pruning, arranging, and loving the earth's most bountiful creations takes a generous and soulful heart. A garden starts off with the same blank wonder as the painter's canvas and the writer's notebook, waiting patiently for its greatest form to reveal itself. Gardens differ, however, in that their care is ongoing, and does not accept its creator to simply walk away when complete.

As homemakers and designers and everything in between, we spend infinite amounts of time crafting and perfecting our houses, apartments, condos, and cabins to nurture our every need. At least, that is what I am hoping you will do after reading this book. But there remains a crucial, enchanting world outside of your home

....

27. Goodreads. "Mary Cantwell Quotes," accessed June 2021, www.goodreads .com/quotes/marycantwell.

that has the possibility of uplifting your well-being beyond measure: the gardens.

If a formal garden is not something you have where you live now, worry not, because any space you can cultivate outside and use for yourself will be magic, even a small balcony housing your collection of herbs, flowerpots, or tropical plants over the summer.

From a spiritual perspective, working with the earth is a fundamental part of a healthy inner life. No matter what your schedule looks like, or how many kids, pets, and jobs you have, taking the time to tend a garden or a few plants will have far reaching impacts on your sense of connectivity to this planet. The health benefits of gardening are well documented, and not only can you experience stress relief from playing with flowers, but you might also gain a greater sense of the world around you. Spending time with the natural world is enriching because it reminds us that we are not the center of the universe, and that there exists so much more living, growing and thriving forms of energy outside of our ego driven bodies.

My youngest daughter began growing apple seeds for a homeschooling project last year, and the immense appreciation for being able to tend to something, watch it change, and come to understand the cycle of growing food has been a profound lesson for us both. We all need these reminders from time to time, when grabbing prepared food becomes mindless and we no longer stop to think about the magic of the process and the potential of every single seed. The miracle of life tends to dissipate somewhere in the daily grind when our routines do not involve working with the land and cultivating our own sustenance.

If you practice a pagan religion, you are undoubtedly already overflowing with plant life, indoors and out. But regardless of your spiritual orientation, many people feel the pull of greenspace, whether to grow their own food, attract the birds, bees, and butterflies, or simply to enjoy a couple of months of fresh and fragrant blooms.

Whatever space you do have to work with, follow the tips below for creating an intuitive outdoor space for restoration, play, harmony, or even magic.

Balconies

Starting small, balconies are tons of fun when crafting an outdoor greenspace and one of my all-time favorite design challenges. Apartments, condos, and large family homes have balconies, so this is an area everyone can play around with and test out their space planning skills. But even if you do only have a tiny space to work with, do not let it go to waste. Many apartments and condos lack a surrounding abundance of trees, so make an impact by adding some beauty and natural elegance to what you have.

If you do become stuck for ideas as to how to pull this off, the internet offers some exceptionally crafty visuals for small balconies that I highly recommend looking for. I never cease to be amazed at the ingenuity of the human mind when it comes to transforming space; to turn an eight-foot box into a paradise is truly a creative feat we can emulate anywhere.

To begin your balcony transformation, start by giving it a good overhaul and clean it. This should always be where you start, no matter what space you are working with and sets the energetic foundation of what you are planning to build. Wash the deck, paint the siding, pressure wash the railings. Spring is a perfect time for this exercise to wash away the molds and dead debris from the fall and winter months. Try the meditation exercise at the end of this chapter for calling in new, fresh energies from the earth and to honor the cycle of rebirth.

Now, start your outdoor greenspace with somewhere cozy to sit. If you're going to soak up all that newness of the spring and summer months, you should be comfortable at least. Most balconies will fit a bistro set, but if you plan to really relax out there try an outdoor lounger, an armchair with ottoman, or create your own seating with a well-dressed mattress on pallets—a popular Pinterest idea as well! Do not forget to add a table for that cup of morning coffee or evening tea and a few pillows and blankets for an extra dose of luxury.

Once you have your basic seating outlined you can assess the space for your plant life. Have a combination of sizes going, from potted trees and shrubs to starter plants to planter boxes. As every plant will have different sunlight requirements, choose plants carefully to adapt to the light available in your chosen space. If you get no direct sun, go for greens and blooms that do well in the shade or indirect light. A deck full of dying plants is bad feng shui, and a terrible waste of moola.

If you are hoping to attract some amazing little pollinators, like butterflies, hummingbirds, and bumblebees, get to know the favorites and turn your little patch of heaven into a lively, bustling metropolis. This goes for any outdoor garden space, where a little careful planning will bring you endless hours of birdwatching enjoyment. Adding bird feeders might help draw them in also, and I can attest firsthand to the dramatic daily meanderings of my resident hummingbirds and their gusto at defending their turf year-round. Dodging a territorial hummingbird chasing competition at thirty mph at eye level is terrifying, but completely *amazing* and why you need to try it.

One of the best ways of filling that teeny tiny balcony space with overflowing plant life is to add wall planters. Wooden pallets or slats are an easy DIY option, as are metal racks or shelving. Pick a side of your balcony that is enclosed and go from bottom to top, creating depth and interest. You can also get crafty and find ways to suspend those dangling plants and flower baskets from the roof, adding a bit of jungle feel to your cozy little Eden.

Another great addition to small balcony areas is well-chosen outdoor lighting. White string lights, or fairy lights, are always a magical choice illuminating your newfound haven with a soft and enchanting glow. Outdoor lanterns also add the same kind of whimsy, or anything that recreates the gentle warmth of candlelight.

Backyards

If the place you call home is blessed with some greenspace, you have a great opportunity to start connecting with those green thumbs. Not everyone enjoys the regular maintenance of grass cutting, weed whacking, or weeding out flower beds, though, as you found out in the very first part of the book. But if you're one of those people that shouted a resounding "yes please!" to having a giant backyard for frolicking and festivities, this section is for you.

Your first task when looking to revamp your outdoor space is to assess how you want to use it. This can be tricky, especially if you've never had a backyard of your very own before, or if you're staring at an endless sea of unmanicured grass boxed in with a private fence. If you have the financial luxury to spend a few bucks on landscaping, you can work out some preliminary plans about how to divide up the space. A flat, uninteresting patch of lawn is great (and certainly more fun than an uninteresting patch of concrete) but could be so much more with the addition of a few layers of garden beds, a rock wall, or even a water feature like a small pond to keep that chi flowing through.

If you have smaller kids, safety will be a priority of course, but you can still divide the space enough to enjoy other non-kid specific activities—like relaxing! Have a place for those kid friendly sandboxes, splash pools, soccer nets, and trampolines but allow yourself the enjoyment of a comfortable seating area, a place for your favorite flowers, and a bird feeding station. Having children does not have to mean a yard full of toys and soccer balls. It's good for them, too, to appreciate tending their own beautiful piece of this earth. Try making homemade wooden signposts for these different "sections" of the backyard. As a family you can have a designated flower garden, veggie patch, sandpit, games zone, or fairy village. Not only does this offer you a way to use your backyard in the ways you want it, but it will also help your little one's respect boundaries and encourage them to join in on the nurturing fun of yard work.

One of the best backyards I ever had was surrounded by berry producing bushes that attracted cedar waxwings. I set up bird feeding sections at all four corners of the yard and a bird bath right in the center. The hummingbirds had corner A, the goldfinches occupied corner B, the chickadees and woodpeckers corner C, and the crows, magpies, and blue jays fought over corner D with a daily treat bowl of peanuts, leftovers, or hotdogs. To my surprise and delight, I had several unexpected guests, such as falcons trying to peg off the songbirds, and one random Canadian goose wandering the path eating stray seeds. Some days needed a traffic control system, and the winged visitors came at the same times every day. To me, it was magical, spiritual, and gave meaning to my outdoor space while I had it.

The key is to find a way to use your outside space in a way that allows you to experience nature personally, and make being out there an organic, uplifting, and restorative endeavor. However, you decide to map out your personal patch of paradise, give it some diversity by adding a combination of trees, flowers, herbs, and homegrown veggies. Remember to do your research about the unique requirements for each species, and group together those with similar needs.

By creating some variety in your backyard, you invite different energies, species, aromas, and magical elements to be savored, shared, and nurtured.

If you're looking for some inspiration for your optimal garden, try following some traditional feng shui tips for maximizing the positive flow of healthy energy into your life. The garden is very important in this ancient practice, and is thought to determine what type of energy, or chi, flows into the home. A well-designed garden is great feng shui. If it makes you feel good and refreshes the senses, then you know you're off to a good start. The chapter on feng shui later in this book will have a few more details and tips for applying to garden settings.

Magical Plants and Flowers

Plants have always been a necessary part of religious traditions, pagan and not. As with every philosophy presented in this book, you do not need to be a believer in anything otherworldly to feel and use the magic of the natural earth elements. Just being alive as an organic being makes you inextricably linked to everything in your garden. You share the same air, the same need for water and sunlight, and the food you eat is nurtured by the same soil as your prized petunias.

Many flowers are also considered medicinal, some even edible, so keeping a healthy garden close by could be a multipurpose endeavor. But just for explorations sake, and for those curious about some more interesting facets of florals and herbs, we will dig a little deeper into what magical folk use those common garden companions for.

A Witch's Garden

Chamomile: A soothing addition to any garden, this flowering herb is beneficial for calming the nerves and enticing a restful night's sleep. Used often in ancient Egypt as a medicinal remedy and enjoyed as a hot beverage by the Romans, this daisy-like flower has been attributed with faster wound healing, stomach soothing, and cold relief. In spell craft, chamomile can be used for protection, healing, purification, and good luck. Plant chamomile close to the front door to banish negativity from entering.

Lavender: My favorite flower, lavender is a potent and hypnotizing friend for any garden, balcony, or sunroom. Used by the Romans to scent just about everything, this versatile member of the mint family induces peace and positive vibes due to its pleasant aroma. Medicinally lavender is used to reduce stress and is also believed to have antiseptic qualities.

Lavender also makes for a trusty companion in the kitchen and its culinary uses worldwide in baking, sauces, teas, honey, and dressings is well established. For magical work or use, this stunning purple flower can be used for protection against negativity and bringing joy and serenity. A sachet full of lavender placed under your pillow may also help with dream magic and a restful night's sleep. Its soothing purple color connects this flower to the crown chakra and will aid in meditation work.

Plant lavender in front of the house, keep vases stuffed with fresh cuts of lavender flowers, or make a lavender wreath to hang on the front door.

Moonflower: A truly magical garden ally, this beautiful white flower is nocturnal, opening up when the evening begins and relishing in the light of the moonlight, releasing its fragrance into the night air. Although this plant is toxic to both human and animal if ingested, it attracts several types of moths to pollinate. Its association with the night has, like the owl, given it some very witchy properties and moonflower has been attributed with transformation magic, shapeshifting, occult mysteries and increasing psychic abilities.

Sunflower: A great garden companion to place beside your moon-flowers, sunflowers epitomize the energy and vitality of the sun. Not only do they impart an immediate sense of happiness to those who see them, they are a favorite food source of many birds, bees, butter-flies, and other small critters, making it a great choice for a bustling flower patch.

Being rich in vitamins A, B, C, and E, sunflower oils are often used for radiant skin and hair, while their delicious seeds are a good source of beneficial fats, proteins, and minerals.

Being associated with the sun, sunflowers represent fertility and have been regarded as emblems of prosperity and good fortune for hundreds of years. Plant sunflowers for a daily dose of positivity, to attract pollinators, and to usher in wealth and bright beginnings.

Sage: Discussed in the chapter on space clearing, sage is another prized member of the mint family used for protection, cleansing, and banishing for centuries. It is prized all over the world for its strong aroma and earthly flavor, making it a great ally in any kitchen and is equipped with loads of antioxidants, vitamins, and minerals.

The most widely used varieties of sage have antimicrobial and antibacterial properties, which means they can keep viruses, bacteria, and fungi at bay. White sage is also great at repelling insects. Incorporated widely throughout the medicinal practices of ancient Egypt, Greece, and Rome, it is still trusted today as a powerful herb for healing. White sage is held sacred among many shamanic and Native American belief systems, where it is believed to dispel negative energies from both the physical and etheric bodies. Use this amazing herb to purify the spiritual body, cleanse the air in any space and rid your home of old unwanted energetic "stuff."

Lemon Balm: An old favorite of mine, and another member of the mint family, lemon balm is one of those plants that grows like wildfire but releases a beautiful lemon aroma into the garden.

When I had bunnies, it was one of their favorite treats and thankfully replenished itself faster than they could eat it. Loved by most gardeners, lemon balm attracts many beneficial pollinators such as bees, butterflies, and even hummingbirds while its strong citrus odor repels mosquitos and gnats.

Believed to be a stress reliever, anti-inflammatory, and antibacterial warrior, this plant makes a soothing tea and a nice refreshing addition to your summer water. In magic, lemon balm is often used in love and healing spells and for manifestation work.

Rosemary: An ancient symbol of remembrance and another plant of the mint family native to the Mediterranean, this fragrant herb has been celebrated since early Greek culture. It is said that Greek scholars would wear garland of rosemary on their heads during exams to aid with memory and they strongly believed it boosted the brain's stamina. Another herb rich in antioxidants and anti-inflammatory compounds, rosemary boasts many health benefits and is thought to boost immunity and aid blood circulation. It is also widely used in the culinary world for soups, stews, and salads and enhances potatoes, poultry, fish, and other game.

In your personal garden, rosemary will add both fragrance and beauty with early blooming flowers. While the strong smell will divert some regular garden pests, it will also attract important pollinators like hummingbirds and bees looking to get a head start in the late winter and early spring.

Rosemary is often used as an incense and can be incorporated into your space clearing festivities and rituals. Said to attract love, fidelity, and protection, add rosemary to an herbal wreath at the front door alongside lavender and sage.

Roses: One of history's most beloved flowers, and an estimated 35 million years old, the rose holds a special place in human history. The queen of all flowers, roses have been used in many cultures throughout the world medicinally and symbolically and play an integral part in many garden arrangements.

Rosewater is a famous treatment for glowing, healthy, and toned skin, calming inflammation and reducing redness. It has been applied for thousands of years to reduce irritation and wrinkles and also appears widely in cosmetics. Rose tea and oil are also popular remedies for many feminine ailments and is often used to treat stomach discomforts. Like many other flowers and herbs in your magical garden, rose also has antibacterial qualities.

Symbolically, roses have very powerful associations and should be celebrated in your outdoor garden spaces. In some religions, the rose represents the soul, while in others it is the eternal love and guidance offered to humanity by the gods. There are many stories throughout history connecting the smell of roses with the visitation of angels and is an indication that the spirit world is sending you messages.

Rose colors represent many things, but if you're going to add some into your garden design consider these common connections. White roses usually signify purity, holiness, and simplicity. Symbols of innocence and chastity, they are often seen at weddings and christenings. Red roses are often connected with passionate love and romance. They are the go-to gift for Valentine's Day and signify the deep stirrings of desire. Pink roses represent a simple joy and happiness and can also convey admiration and gratitude for others. Yellow roses are often symbols of friendship, caring, affection and a simple delight in life and are excellent additions to any garden.

Mint: Although several plants already mentioned belong to the mint family, this section refers to the most familiar of those from the genus *mentha*, mainly peppermint, spearmint and watermint. The word *mint* is rooted in the Latin word *minthe*, who, in Greek mythos was a nymph who was turned into a mint plant by a jealous Persephone, the wife of Hades.

Mint was often used in ancient Greek funerary rites along with other aromatic herbs like rosemary, likely due more to their ability to mask the odors of decaying bodies than anything else. The Romans, too, enjoyed the refreshing qualities of mint and would add it to bathwater and use it to clean teeth, as we still do today.

The Egyptians also made wide use of this soothing herb and made mint a part of their medicinal arsenal, using it for its effectiveness in calming tummy troubles. Peppermint is, in fact, a very carminative substance and has fantastic ability to reduce gas in the body and soothe an upset stomach. It relaxes digestive muscles and aids in producing stomach acid and bile.

Adding peppermint to your garden not only allows the refreshing aroma to wander into your space, but it also keeps an important and effective medicinal ally close at hand. Mint is easy to grow, so make sure you trim it back often, so you do not get overrun.

Because it is such a soothing, refreshing herb, mint is often used for cleansing and banishing negative energy in the home. Try incorporating mint into your space clearing exercises by washing floors with mint water after an argument or to clear out old unwanted patterns. It is also a highly recommended herb for protection and should be planted around the house, or close to the front and back doors.

Mugwort: Perhaps one of the more popular plants in the world of plant magic, mugwort has a variety of uses and medicinal qualities. According to *Garden Culture Magazine*, the botanical name of mugwort, *Artemisia, vulgaris* honors the Greek goddess Artemis. Like its namesake, the plant is associated with the moon, cycles, women's health, and childbirth.[28] In folk medicine, mugwort was used

....

28. Caroline Rivard, "Mugwort: A Magical and Medicinal Weed," *Garden Culture Magazine*, issue 31, March 2020, www.gardenculturemagazine.com.

primarily for relieving menstrual pain and is believed to induce abortion in high amounts.

A member of the daisy family, this versatile flowering herb has been used as a food, spice, spiritual ally, a flavoring for beer and other beverages, and is traditionally used in the Chinese medicinal practice of moxibustion. This healing art has been practiced for more than 3,000 years to stimulate personal qi and expel pathogens from the body. It is also said to have relaxing effects on the mind and body and is commonly used to support digestion. It is also said that the Romans, on their way to battle, placed mugwort in their sandals to prevent foot fatigue.

In terms of more magical purposes, mugwort is used most commonly for astral projection, lucid dreaming and for increasing psychic powers, and among the Celtic Druids, it was a sacred plant thought to ward off evil and poisons.

Thyme: An old, celebrated member of the mint family from the Mediterranean, thyme is a highly aromatic herb equipped with medicinal, ornamental, and dietary qualities. It also has preservative qualities and has long been used to preserve meats and even had its place it ancient Egyptian embalming ceremonies. Thyme also boasts antiseptic properties and was also thought to rid the body of the poisons in ancient times. The Romans found this trait especially useful and added thyme to bath water, as well as a flavoring for food and water.

This flowering herb was also loved by the Greeks and was used freely for incense. The name "thyme," in fact, is a Greek word derived from the words meaning "incense" (*thymiama*), and also the word meaning "bravery or courage" (*thymos* or *thumus*). It is said that Greek soldiers would steep themselves in thyme bathwater to enhance their courage before battle.

Among Pagan circles, thyme is a potent cleansing herb, often used in cleansing baths before rituals, or as a ritual itself. It is believed to rid the aura of past hurts and purify the spirit. Many Pagan practices involved the use of burning thyme to purify space and consecrate altars in preparation for magical works.

Feng Shui for the Garden

The garden is a great escape for many people, whether you are actively toiling over a productive garden or one simply flower filled for the senses. The state of your garden, however, is crucial for overall well-being, luck and success under the feng shui microscope and should be handled with care.

The best way to use your garden to draw in strong, healthy chi is to make sure you're not sitting on a pile of dead matter. A garden that is not tended regularly can quickly fill up with decaying plant materials which can lead to other problems, such as bugs feeding off the rotten plants, and a general poor appearance. I once rented a cute little cabin in the country, swayed by the appeal of a full ocean view. The homeowners, however, left a pile of old firewood outside for about ten years beside an old cedar tree that grew over top of the house. Needless to say, the house was eventually infested by carpenter ants that used the giant tree as a bridge to make their exodus inside my walls. And yes, I moved out.

Never overlook the maintenance of what surrounds your home and the importance of good housekeeping outside. If you have the time and energy to maintain a garden full of plant life, that is great! But if you do not, keep it cleared of anything requiring regular care and opt for a simple grass yard instead, free from clutter and debris.

If you do have a garden, use some feng shui ideas for balancing the elements in your outdoor space. Remember, when applying the bagua map to your home's floorplan, the garden counts too. Depending on where your garden space is located, you will need to be mindful of the elemental energies playing the biggest influence here. In feng shui, plants fall under the element of wood. Wood is nourished by water, and nourishes the fire element. A garden in the southern parts of your house will add excellent life energy to the wealth, family, and fame sectors on your bagua map.

Adding a water feature is also considered one of the most important aspects of a garden and the best way to add positive, life affirming chi to your home. Water symbolizes wealth in feng shui as well as strong nourishing energy. A fountain that pours water will create a peaceful quality as well as boost your water element energy. If you're into obsessive bird watching like me, a water feature is a sure way to attract the winged ones to your yard alongside all those bursting flower pots.

Some other garden tips:

Add bird feeders. Inviting birds into your garden adds a special kind of energy. In feng shui, and pretty much everywhere, birds represent freedom and will bring some fresh, swooping vibrant energy to your outdoor space.

Add windchimes. Windchimes are an easy way to add the element of metal and add delightful sounds to fill the senses. What better way to witness energy flow through your garden than to watch it make music for you?

Make a pathway. Many gardens done according to the principles of feng shui incorporate paths that allow the easy meandering through the flowers on a summer afternoon. Go for curvy pathways instead of longer straight ones to slow down the moving energy and create a sense of calm.

Add seating. Discussed in our chapter on garden spaces, adding a few comfortable places to sit is the perfect way to invite yourself and others a chance to sit and relax in the refreshing outdoors.

Make sure your seating choices are in good repair and replace any old chairs that have been weather damaged or otherwise worn out. Keeping those old, dilapidated deck chairs you've had for ten years might not be the best feng shui when nobody wants to have a seat and enjoy themselves.

Crystals for the Garden

Clear quartz is a great addition to an outdoor setting because of its ability to create those magical rainbows when the sun shines through them. But all crystals would be welcome in the garden to boost and mingle with the vibrant energies of the plant life, insect and bird life, and all of those natural elements working together in perfectly designed bliss.

Deities for the Garden

Brownie: Like the Nisse of the Nordic folktales, the brownie is a popular house spirit in the Scottish folk history who acts as a guardian of the home, doing household and farm chores as it pleases him. They will ensure the prosperity of the family and household if they are kept happy and expect an offering of porridge or milk daily.

The brownie is said to be a derivative of the old ancestor cults, like the Lares of ancient Rome, which focused heavily on the hearth as the center of familial life and worship and began as tutelary domestic deities. Brownies are usually described as ugly creatures, about the size of children like the Nisse, with brown skin, hairy bodies and either seen naked or in rag clothing. The best way to offend a brownie, apparently, is to offer him clothing, doing so will anger him to the extent he will leave the home forever.

Nisse: Also known as Tomte, these little folk in Scandinavian tradition were believed to live secretly in the home and act as its guardian. They were particularly fond of farm animals and children, and if treated well, they would keep a diligent watch that no evils or misfortunes would fall upon them. Nisse were also apt to help with chores around the farm but were easily offended and would retaliate against a family and homestead if any disrespect was shown to the Nisse or the farmstead itself. They were also associated with the winter solstice and Yule and were even believed to bring gifts to children. The Nordic people would leave offerings of food for the house Nisse to keep him happy and ensure good fortune for the home.

The normal appearance of a Nisse is said to be that of a very small, bearded old man, dressed in a farmer's clothing. In modern-day Denmark, the Nisse is depicted as beardless and wearing a red cap.

EXERCISE
Meditation for a Restorative Garden

For those of you inclined to see the symbolic side of life, this next meditation will be quite simple. The garden has long been used as a metaphor for life, and in particular, the state of our minds and our lives. Seeds can be visualized as our thoughts, being planted into the garden of our lives and it is up to us whether we turn those seeds into flowers, weeds, or nothing at all. If we really focus on this metaphorically, the weeds can be seen as everyday thoughts that tend to crowd our minds and take over the garden if we are not paying attention. These could be anxieties, fears, wants, wishes, regrets. If we want to grow flowers—the sweet smelling, beautiful roses of our existence which might be joy, peace, love and acceptance—we need to tend to our inner gardens diligently and effectively.

It seems easier to give our minds over to the weeds, for some oddly dark reason, and forget that we have the same power to grow the roses that we have to grow anything else. Use these visuals in the following exercise to maximize the emotional and spiritual impact your physical garden might have on your inner world.

Get comfortable. Try and do this meditation outside if you can, in the area you are cultivating or preparing for a garden, or an existing garden space. Have some flowers and plants around you and have at least one hand on the dirt. Imagine the richness of the soil. Visualize the nutrients it supplies to everything living thing on earth. Think about the bugs that keep it moving and healthy, the weeds, herbs, trees, flowers, fruits, and vegetables that grow from seed within it. See also the herbivores that eat the flora and go all the way up the food chain to humanity, nourished by every facet of everything that springs forth from that earth.

Once you have that connection grounded inside of you, start to visualize your garden. Imagine planting new seeds into that soil which represent the things you hold dear and wish to grow in your life. Good health, love, money, opportunity, success. Plant these seeds in your garden and feel their deepness in the ground.

Go through the entire visualization of seeing that seed accept the sun, accept the water and begin to sprout. Imagine that as each one of these seeds turns into a living, thriving plant, your dreams and hopes grow alongside them. See the opening and blooming of each flower manifest your hopes and become joyful and abundant life experiences. Feel the warmth of the sun as the confirmation of a successful life.

Now visualize the birds, butterflies, bees and other insects being nurtured in return by the fullness of your manifestations. See the connections between *your* abundance and your ability to share it with others. Your garden is full of new life, and it spills over into the lives of those around you. The energy of your garden flows into every facet of your life and the world around you in small, but very meaningful ways.

When you have completed this visualization, thank the earth for the endless abundance she provides each moment of your life. Hold in your thoughts a few of the things you cherish about the home you tend on this planet, and how grateful you are to have a place of your own.

Conclusion

....

Transforming your home into a place where life happens can be, and *should* be, a magical experience. As you have learned from this book, people have always found meaningful ways to adapt personal space and honor the energies that have nurtured them—whatever force they believed was behind the magic.

But achieving this sense of home is primarily a subjective endeavor. No matter which schools of design, religions, or philosophies you choose to take your cues from, the end result comes from you and the intentions you put into molding your home and life journey. No design trend will ever capture the spiritual needs of everyone, just as no religion or spiritual doctrine could ever cater to the whole of humanity. We are all different, and we all respond to the environments around us in unique ways. This is where I see the largest gap between the hugely popular interior design industry and the pushing quest for more personal and spiritual spaces. While there are many amazing designers paving the way for a more organic approach to design and architecture, there still lingers the ideal of a trendsetting mentality that pushes a cookie cutter way of building and furnishing homes. There are those out there who enjoy the fads and the thrill of jumping onto the proverbial bandwagon. But for those of you who want a home more handcrafted, more finely tuned, now is your chance to merge a sincere self-exploration with your interior refresh project.

In venturing into the domain of transforming your space into your perfect home, I encourage you to explore a bit of everything until you find what feels right for you and your family. Try the color exercises, the meditations, and grab a compass to give the feng shui a shot. You may even find another approach that works better for you outside of everything I have written about. Whatever road you choose for your unique home optimizing endeavors I hope it brings you profound joy and that you truly and genuinely find your way home.

Recommended Reading

....

Barrett, Jayme. *Feng Shui Your Life: Second Edition*. New York: Sterling Ethos, 2012.

Carter, Karen Rauch. *Move Your Stuff, Change Your Life: How to Use Feng Shui to Get Love, Money, Respect and Happiness*. New York: Simon and Schuster, 2000.

Gaines, Joanna. *Homebody: A Guide to Creating Spaces You Never Want to Leave*. New York: Harper Design, 2018.

Henson, Emily, and Ryland Peters and Small. *Modern Rustic: Relaxed Rooms for Easy Living*. 2021.

Kondo, Marie. *The Life-Changing Magic of Tidying Up: The Japanese Art of Decluttering and Organizing*. Ten Speed Press, 2014

Mayer, Lee and Emily Motayed. *Design the Home You Love: Practical Styling Advice to Make the Most of Your Space*. Berkley, CA: Ten Speed Press, 2021.

McAllister, Colin and Justin Ryan. *Escapology: Modern Cabins, Cottages and Retreats*. Vancouver: Figure 1 Publishing, 2020.

Whitehurst, Tess. *Magical Housekeeping: Simple Charms and Practical Tips for Creating a Harmonious Home*. Woobury, MN: Llewellyn Publications, 2010.

Bibliography

Boechler, Ethan, Allison Campbell, Jordan Hanania, James Jenden, Jason Donev. "Energy Education: Law of conservation of energy." Last updated September 27, 2021. https://energyeducation.ca/encyclopedia/Law_of_conservation_of_energy.

Bryson, Bill. *At Home: A Short History of Private Life.* New York: Doubleday, 2010.

Burn, Shawn M. "The Trouble with Houseguests." Psychology Today. Last updated July 25, 2013. www.psychologytoday.com/ca/blog/presence-mind/201307/the-trouble-houseguests.

Conservation Center, The. "Pigment of the Month: Vermillion." Last updated August 28, 2019. http://www.theconservationcenter.com/articles/2019/8/28/pigment-of-the-month-vermilion.

Cousins, Carrie. "Colour and Cultural Design Considerations." Colours & Materials. Last updated November 7, 2014. https://

coloursandmaterials.wordpress.com/2014/11/07
/colour-and-cultural-design-considerations/.

Dowdey, Sarah. "How Smell Works." How Stuff Works. Last
updated October 29, 2007. https://health.howstuffworks.com
/mental-health/human-nature/perception/smell.htm.

Goodreads. "Mary Cantwell Quotes." Accessed June 2021. www
.goodreads.com/quotes/marycantwell.

Graham, Helen. *Discover Colour Therapy*. Berkeley, CA: Ulysses
Press; 1998.

Grovier, Kelly. "The Murky History of the Colour Yellow." *BBC*.
Last updated September 6, 2018. https://www.bbc.com
/culture/article/20180906-did-animal-cruelty-create
-indian-yellow.

Hill, J. "Colour: Green." Ancient Egypt Online. Last updated 2010.
https://ancientegyptonline.co.uk/colourgreen/2010.

Ireland Calling. "Brigid's Cross (Brighid's Cross, St. Brigit's Cross)."
Accessed February 2021. https://ireland-calling.com
/brigids-cross.

Jiang, Fercility. "Lucky Colors in China." China Highlights. Last
updated December 1, 2021. https://www.chinahighlights.com
/travelguide/culture/lucky-numbers-and-colors-in-chinese
-culture.htm.

Lasner, Matthew. *High Life: Condo Living in the Suburban Century*.
New Haven, CT: Yale University Press, 2012.

Lowe, Andy. "Why is the color blue so rare in nature?" The University of Adelaide. Last updated August 20 2019. https://sciences.

adelaide.edu.au/news/list/2019/08/20
/why-is-the-colour-blue-so-rare-in-nature.

MacDonald, Fiona. "There's Evidence Humans Didn't Actually See Blue Until Modern Times." Science Alert. Last updated April 7, 2018. https://www.sciencealert.com/humans-didn-t-see-the-colour-blue-until-modern-times-evidence-science.

Máchal, Jan. "Slavic Mythology" In *The Mythology of All Races. III, Celtic and Slavic Mythology*, edited by L.H. Gray. Boston: Wentworth Press, 1918.

Mark, Joshua J. "Vesta." World History Encyclopedia. Last updated September 2, 2009. https://www.worldhistory.org/Vesta/.

McAllister, Colin and Justin Ryan. *Escapology: Modern Cabins, Cottages and Retreats*. Vancouver: Figure.1 Publishing, 2020.

Olesen, Jacob. "The Rarest and Most Expensive Colors in the World Throughout History." Color Meanings. Last updated 2021. https://www.color-meanings.com/rare-expensive-colors-world-history/ 2021.

Pokorska, Anna. "Colors of Ancient Egypt: Red." London's Global University Blogs. Last updated December 4, 2018. https://blogs.ucl.ac.uk/researchers-in-museums/2018/12/04/colours-of-ancient-egypt-red/.

Pollard, Amanda . "How to Design a Home That Boosts Well-Being." Houzz. Last updated November 7, 2020. https://www.houzz.com/magazine/how-to-design-a-home-that-boosts-well-being-stsetivw-vs~128031623.

Racoma, Bernadine. "Color Symbolism—Psychology Across Cultures." Day Translations Blog. Last updated July 26, 2019. https://www.daytranslations.com/blog/color-psychology/.

Rivard, Caroline. "Mugwort: A Magical and Medicinal Weed." *Garden Culture Magazine*, Issue 31, March 2020. www.gardenculturemagazine.com.

Science History Institute. "William Henry Perkin." Last updated December 14, 2017. https://www.sciencehistory.org/historical-profile/william-henry-perkin.

Stewart, Jessica. "The History of the Colour Orange: From Tomb Paintings to Modern Day Jumpsuits." My Modern Met. Last updated February 21, 2019. https://mymodernmet.com/history-color-orange.

Stewart, Susan. "Reading a Drawer." *Room One Thousand*, 2 (2014): 14–30. https://escholarship.org/uc/item/4t87g8bw.

Webb, Mary. *The Spring of Joy: A Little Book of Healing*. London and Toronto: J.M Dent and Sons Ltd., New York: E.P Dutton and Co., 1917.

To Write to the Author

If you wish to contact the author or would like more information about this book, please write to the author in care of Llewellyn Worldwide Ltd. and we will forward your request. Both the author and publisher appreciate hearing from you and learning of your enjoyment of this book and how it has helped you. Llewellyn Worldwide Ltd. cannot guarantee that every letter written to the author can be answered, but all will be forwarded. Please write to:

Lesley A. Morrison
℅ Llewellyn Worldwide
2143 Wooddale Drive
Woodbury, MN 55125-2989

Please enclose a self-addressed stamped envelope for reply,
or $1.00 to cover costs. If outside the U.S.A., enclose
an international postal reply coupon.

Many of Llewellyn's authors have websites with additional information and resources. For more information, please visit our website at http://www.llewellyn.com

Notes

Notes

Notes

Notes